SHADOWLANDS

Expanding Being-becoming beyond Liminality, Crossroads and Borderlands

Edited by
Remi Calleja

Langaa Research & Publishing CIG
Mankon, Bamenda

Publisher:

Langaa RPCIG
Langaa Research & Publishing Common Initiative Group
P.O. Box 902 Mankon
Bamenda
North West Region
Cameroon
Langaagrp@gmail.com
www.langaa-rpcig.net

Distributed in and outside N. America by African Books Collective
orders@africanbookscollective.com
www.africanbookscollective.com

ISBN-10: 9956-551-87-2

ISBN-13: 978-9956-551-87-3

Notes on Contributors

Remi Calleja, an anthropology researcher at UCT, centred his Master research on the process of identity negotiation among a group of Capetonian Bush Doctors. After completing his undergraduate in anthropology at University Aix-Marseille, France, he was able to narrow down his centres of interest which encompass the fields of identity negotiation and formation, Indigenous knowledge, as well as traditional medicine and spiritualities.

Charne Parrott did her undergraduate degree at Rhodes University. She continued her studies at UCT and focused on multispecies ethnography, an approach that proposes to understand the complex and interconnected relations composing the web of life. This perspective unveils new potentialities for thinking the social/biological divisions.

Simone Oosthuizen was a central contributor in the framing of the shadowlands. She helped imagining and coordinating the project throughout the Ethnographic Problematics course. This course emerged as the initial space in which the group of contributors united.

Irinja Vähäkangas, from Finland, undertook her anthropology Master at UCT in 2018. Alongside her classmates, she greatly contributed to shaping the concept of shadowlands.

Lindela Mjenxane contributed to the framing and writing of the introductory chapter of this volume. We acknowledge his input with gratitude.

Finally, this work could not have been carried out without the teachings and wit of Professor Francis Nyamnjoh. Dr.

Nyamnjoh has published extensively on globalisation, media, citizenship, and the politics of identity in Africa. Introducing the students to Amos Tutuola and emphasising on incompleteness, mobility, and fluidity in the process of identity negotiation, Dr Nyamnjoh provided the building blocks in the framing of the project that has resulted in this publication.

Table of Contents

Preface

Anthropology is no stranger to the need to make new concepts or to the practice of watching permutations as old ones travel into new terrains. Throughout its history it has crisscrossed the world, trafficking signs and their relations to world-making practices, seeking ways to make multiple forms of life legible across difference. Our work as translators, brokers and crafters of new knowledge involves thinking carefully about how concepts work, whether they are transferable from the contexts in which they were generated and have life, and if so, what their effects are. That its efforts have been saturated in power relations is not in question; that we may miss the mark and in so doing do injustice is clear.

Some of Anthropology's oldest and richest anthropological questions and concepts are drawn from worlds unfamiliar to European scholars who sought to describe and analyse lives far from what were then considered the metropoles. Think for example of the Māori word '*hau*' whose genealogy in anthropology comes to us through Marcel Mauss's (1954) writings on the gift. In Mauss's famous formulation, the gift, while it appears disinterested in the sense of being freely given without expectation of return, contains an essence that draws from others an inevitable response. He uses '*hau*', a Māori term to describe this 'spirit' of the gift. From this was born one of anthropology's most enduring problematics, to do with how politics, economics and social life enfold one another and solidarities are created. Mauss's argumentation gave rise to careful thought about the nature of the gift, the question of reciprocity, the forms and limits of social solidarity. For Mauss, the spirit of the gift – the way that it produced an endless moral cycle of prestation and return – was the foundation of human sociality. Entering into one of sociology's most influential texts on economics and politics, the Māori term has taken on a new life, inserted into modes of reason about political organisation and policy. The debates it produced have not ended; the problem of reciprocity and altruism – of the gift – circles in multiple fields, particularly most recently in relation to questions of the alienability of human body parts through organ and fluid donation. Underpinning all of this, is a term drawn from indigenous life worlds and rendered as a concept.

Hau received a further permutation when the journal and master series of the same name was introduced in 2011. That resource offers reproductions of 'master texts' with contemporary commentaries and a thematic journal, with the intention of '… situating ethnography as the primary heuristic of anthropology and returning it to the forefront of conceptual developments in the discipline' (HAU 2011). Ironically, the journal claims the source of its name as Mauss's *The Gift* with no acknowledgment of the indigenous world from which the concept was wrested in the first instance, notwithstanding HAU's intention to examine translational equivocations that arise in the encounter between 'western cosmological assumptions and conceptual determinations' (ibid) and indigenous knowledge systems. The elision of the primary source of the concept matters, as members of Mahi Tahi, a collective operating under the auspices of the New Zealand Anthropology Association, gently point out.

In an open letter to the journal, Mahi Tahi and a long

list of supporters note that the term '*hau*' was used without discussion or reference to its Māori roots. In an open and reflective mode of engagement, the collective poses questions about whether the journal has lived up to the values of the life worlds from which the term originates. It describes these values as care, respect, openness and inclusivity (2018b). The response itself is characterised by these values; it is not accusatory, unlike much of the social media frenzy that surrounded the debate about editorial practices at the journal, but respectfully draws attention to the values that animate indigenous concepts and relationships. Mahi Tahi draws attention to the appropriation of terms and the lack of consultation but does not make a nativist claim that concepts must remain in the life worlds from which they originate. Rather, the collective suggests that as they travel, their users have a responsibility to ensure that the set of values – let's call them the spirit – of the term moves too and animates the relations it constellates.

Mahi Tahi's short open letter and a follow-up response to HAU's very brief acknowledgement and apology are powerful interventions. In the follow-up response, the collective notes, '… it's worth our whole discipline reflecting on the process by which concepts can get so removed from the communities which generate them'. The point is critical. As our concepts circulate, often far from their sources in life worlds or in theory, they take on lives of their own, generating momentum, accumulating histories, taking unexpected trajectories, showing up in unusual places. Often this is accusingly called 'cultural appropriation'. Mahi Tahi's engagement with HAU initiates a different discussion about what happens when knowledge from one place is taken up elsewhere and gains vital force of its own. While it recognises the appropriative nature of much scholarly thought, Mahi Tahi's responses afford an opening for thought and pose, with great generosity, the question of how we should proceed to value and use ideas and concepts whose theoretical genealogies are entangled with histories of Empire and which continue to live in everyday world-making practices. As we grapple with issues raised in decolonisation debates, these are pointers to a careful thinking through of our conceptual inheritances and what we do with them.

'Concepts', Laura Ann Stoler remarks, 'emerge as seductive and powerful agents' (2016: 8). The claim, offered in a tone that suggests this to be self-evident, should give pause given that we are accustomed to thinking of concepts as tools for thought rather than as agentive in themselves. Yet, as she shows, concepts shape how we think and what we do when we think. Her work, parsing the present for the ways that it enfolds possibilities to 'think otherwise' (Foucault in Stoler 2016: 9), speaks specifically to 'concept-work' (p. 17), an attentiveness to concepts, their manifestation and histories. Concept work, she proposes, 'is more than a methodological invitation; it is an alert, a challenge and a political demand' (ibid). Attentiveness involves noticing what concepts do and what they occlude; what they carry and what they smuggle; what their histories are and what they purport to be. She draws on Foucault's notion of 'mobile thought' (ibid), which she argues 'entails keeping the concepts with which we work provisional, active and subject to change; it entails retaining them both as mobile and as located as they are in the world' (p. 19). We can see these processes at work in the hau/HAU/Mahi Tahi example above, in which a concept was unbedded from everyday practices, re-embedded as a key term in a comparative sociology, contested and engaged. It retains a place both in specific Māori life worlds and in the life worlds of anthropologists and Anthropology, and doubly so where those overlap, as in the Mahi Tahi case. It is both a relational ontology and a material entity circulating text and knowledge practices. And it is brought back into a mutual relation by the engagement of those who represent both Māori and Anthropology. This suggests to me that concepts have vital roles – vital in the sense of living, not only in the sense of important. And this calls on imaginative sensibilities to explore possibilities, limits, constraints and openings.

For Bhrigupati Singh, concepts are both ordinary language and philosophical terms (2014: 182). His point is that the distinction between philosophy and the everyday too often made to valorise the former over the latter simply does not hold. Elsewhere, he proposes that 'Concepts are not dispassionately objective or world ordering. The world is far in excess of our concepts of it' (2015: 2). Later, he notes that 'Our concepts may also be limiting and force us to convey much less than what we saw and felt' (2015: 284). These insights are important for they allow us to consider how concepts are made, what forms of allegiance they entail or inhibit and for whom. 'What, then,' Singh puzzles, 'does a concept offer to ethnographic enquiry?' He answers his question thus: 'It can shift or revise the locus of our hopes or disappointments. As crucially, a concept gives us coordinates along which to pay closer attention' (2014: 168).

The anthropological endeavour, at least on one reading, is an attempt to be attentive to the unfolding of everyday life and to the translational practices that enable that process to become legible across difference. The problem that the authors of this collection address has to do with an overreliance in Anthropology on concepts that reify and fix complex phenomena. Trying to explore the tricky interstices of global modernities, they have turned to classic anthropological concepts, but their analytic work suggests that these concepts contain in their kernel the presuppositions of place and order that characterise Eurocentric theoretical concerns. Order, structure and categorisation are implied in these spatialised concepts, so that the concepts themselves are freighted with assumptions that took form in specific social, intellectual and historical conditions. What then should be done? Drawing on works from across the world, and in particular dialogue with Chicana thought, the authors suggest that we excavate a priori assumptions to see how concepts set in place constellations of ideas that misrecognise experience and make presumptions about reality that might not do justice to the worlds they purport to describe. They have developed a concept of 'shadowlands' to do the analytic work of exploring human adaptability and world-making practices that, they suggest, other concepts, such as liminality, boundaries and borders, leave incomplete or misrecognised. Shadowlands are those shifting spaces that lie beyond, just out of reach of, the concrete facts of dispossessions and erasures of historical and contemporary global modernities.

The authors have taken shadows as inspiration. Let us look more closely at this idea. Picture yourself among trees or in a city. The shadows that surround you are relational. They may be rooted or anchored or grounded, but they change as a result of the movement of light and their relation to other entities around them. As more trees grow or buildings are built, as people and creatures and forces such as wind and rain move among them, the shape of shadows and their connections to others shift. As the light waxes and wanes, shadows alter size, density, shape and length. They track the environment in particular ways, and they do so in relation to both space and time. Of course, shadows and more so, the idea of them, presupposes a solid object that can block light such that patterns emerge. I am thinking here, for example, of shadow puppetry, a centuries old and widespread form of artistry that presents viewers with powerful imagery through skilled use of light, screens and cut-out figures. This suggests that a concept drawing on shadows as inspiration, metaphor and material must make reference to hard facts. In the usage here, however, materiality and the facticity of the world themselves are in question. Ideas of the essential incompleteness of human sociality (Nyamnjoh 2017; see also Biehl and Locke 2017) are set alongside questions of the forces that shape contemporary worlds (Adam Smith's 'invisible hand' is present to be sure, but also the forces that affect us, often unknowingly (see Stewart 2007) or those on which we might call (see Nhemachena 2017) to encourage readers to think more broadly than categorically. The result is a collection of essays that proffer and vitalise a concept. They do not do so uniformly or consistently. One might see the inconsistencies in usage as resulting from poor definition, or one might, as I do, see it as the result of a concept in play, finding its way into a more settled but never finished nature. In this, we might suggest that the concept's use itself plays with the definitions it offers; shifting, changing, not fully fixed. The result is a challenge to an overly settled anthropological thought.

I end this brief preface with questions raised by Mahi Tahi's engagement with the editors of *HAU*. What forms of generosity might our scholarship put in place by thinking alongside the histories of our concepts? What might be the effects of such generosities in reshaping worlding potentialities in the devastating present and the futures it heralds? How might our concepts better honour the diverse world-making practices we come to know?

Fiona C. Ross
Professor of Anthropology
University of Cape Town
June 2019

References

Beihl, J. and Locke, P. (2017) *Unfinished: the anthropology of becoming*, Durham: Duke University Press.

HAU (2011) https://www.haujournal.org/index.html, (last accessed 12 June 2019).

Mahi Tahi (2018a) An Open Letter to the HAU Journal's Board of Trustees. https://www.asaanz.org/blog/2018/6/18/an-open-letter-to-the-hau-journals-board-of-trustees, (last accessed 12 June 2019).

------(2018b) A response and second Open Letter to the Hau Journal's Board of Trustees. https://www.asaanz.org/blog/2018/6/21/a-response-and-

second-open-letter-to-the-hau-journals-board-of-trustees, (last accessed 12 June 2019).
Mauss, M. (2002 [1954]) *The Gift*, London: Routledge.
Nhemachena, A. (2017) *Relationality and Resilience in a Not So Relational World*, Bamenda: Langaa Research and Publishing CIG.
Nyamnjoh, F. (2017) 'Incompleteness. Frontier Africa and the Currency of Conviviality', *Journal of Asian and African Studies*, Vol. 52, No. 3, pp. 253–70.
Singh, B. (2014) 'How Concepts Make the World Look Different: Affirmative and Negative Genealogies of Thought', in V. Das, M. Jackson, A. Kleinman and B Singh (eds), *The Ground Between: Anthropologists Engage Philosophy*, Duke University Press: Durham, pp. 159–86.
------(2015) Poverty and the Quest for Life – Spiritual and Material Striving in Rural India, Chicago: University of Chicago Press.
Stoler, A. L. (2016) 'Critical Incisions: On concept work and colonial recursions', in A. L. Stoler, *Duress: Imperial Durabilities in Our Time,* Durham: Duke University Press.
Stewart, K. (2007) *Ordinary Affects,* Durham: Duke University Press.

Chapter 1

Introduction: Expanding Being-becoming beyond Liminality, Crossroads and Borderlands

R. Calleja, L. Mjenxane, S. Oosthuizen, C. Parrott and I. Vähäkangas

Concepts and theorisation are dynamic, evolving and constant works in progress. Crucial within a specific context, they potentially become inaccurate with time and in different spaces. The metaphorical conceptualisation, as well as the epistemological frameworks of liminality, crossroads and borderlands are no exception to this conceptual plasticity. Therefore, the authors of this book consider the aforementioned metaphors confined and focused primarily on a particular form of being or becoming. This book embarks on reconsidering and expanding on the notion of being, becoming and being-becoming that manifests across the literature of liminality, crossroads and borderlands. The authors intend to overcome eventual limitations of the prior theorisation, in hand with the notions of unfinishedness and incompleteness, to unveil new possibilities in analysis and ethnographic work. The expansion of being, becoming and being-becoming furthers potentialities of analysis and understanding. The metaphor of the shadowlands is, therefore, proposed to accumulate this expansion in an analytical tool. Throughout this book, the authors attempt to move away from the binaries that are perpetuated by the concepts of liminality, crossroads and borderlands. In previous work, processes of being and becoming are often understood as separate processes. While the idea of becoming is characterised by its fluidity, being can be conceived as a static state. In conjunction with unfinishedness and incompleteness, the authors propose that the constant state of becoming can be a state of being, also fluid in nature, introducing the idea of being-becoming and the incomplete being. Being-becoming, therefore, emerges as the project of understanding the two formerly clearly distinct concepts as enmeshed, interdependent and characterised by ideas of dynamism and fluidity. The experience of being-becoming is as an unfinished experience, a space of constant potential renewals and possibilities. In this book, the distinction between being, becoming and being-becoming is utilised to illustrate how being and becoming are grappled within the concepts of liminality, crossroads and borderlands, and how being-becoming and the incomplete being are emphasised in the understanding of the shadowlands.

This introductory chapter embarks on the task outlined above by briefly addressing the genealogies and definitions of the selected grounding concepts: liminality, crossroads and borderlands. Subsequently, in the sections titled Metaphors and Linearity and Direction it moves on to discuss the relevance of metaphors for conceptual work. It does this particularly in relation to the implications of the spatial metaphor and the use of lines in determining the trajectory of movement implied in each of the core concepts employed throughout this work. Stemming from this discussion, the Introduction moves on to analyse the ways in which both the genealogy and the metaphorical manifestation of these concepts inform the intertwining notions of being and becoming therein, before briefly addressing what these mean in the context of the forms of structure and agency prescribed by them. Thereafter, in order to begin bridging the gap between previous conceptual work and the concept of the shadowlands proposed, the section titled Unfinished and Incomplete attempts to begin unpacking the immensely valuable contribution of seeking to see beyond expectations of completeness, wholeness and singularity, and opting to rather envision forms of intermeshed and entangled being-becoming through the prism of perpetual incompleteness. Lastly, the final sections of this chapter function to fuse the various critiques and perspectives which have emerged through this inquiry by introducing the conceptual metaphor of the shadowlands and propose its applicability for both anthropological research and as a tool for anthropological introspection.

Grounding concepts

The concept of liminality was constructed within the context of determining a pattern to the ritual process of a society. Thus, the concept is structured in a step-by-step manner, which sees the liminal persons move from one state of being to another. Turner (1969), who built on Arnold van Gennep's work (1909), distinguishes the liminal venture into three phases. Upon entering the liminal space, the liminal persons, or threshold people, are stripped of the manifestation of their status, which constitutes an integrative part of their identity, and imagined to be a clean state. On an imaginary level, this cleansing of the initial social status allows for openness to all influence. Thereafter, in this ambiguous position, the liminal persons undergo a social transformation, moving from one status to another and eventually assuming another way of being in society.

The final phase in the liminal experience is one of 'reincorporation' (Turner 1969: 94). The liminal persons manoeuvre from the margins and are reintroduced into society with new characteristics shaping their identity, with a new social status that eventually contributes to their new state of being. A crucial point to the reincorporation is the interplay of recognition between the liminal persons and the structured persons. In order to leave liminality, the structured society has to acknowledge the new being, which is done by the attainment of specific social markers. This process illustrates the unilinear trajectory of events within the ritual process, where the outcome is known, and the person progressing into the liminal phase may be stripped of their status and hierarchy but they are fully aware of what is to be achieved by this process. Therefore, the only movement within a liminal experience is forward. Although, some scholars do theorise the possibility of a permanent or sustained liminality (Szakolczai 2000), the outcome of the liminal process is still a linear movement, from one status to another. Similarly, the structure of the three phases, which is also demarcated with social markers, fixes the liminal process with a clear beginning and end.

Although the term itself might not seem to be a metaphor, the concept of liminality stems from the root word '*limen*', translated as the threshold (Turner 1969). The Latin root of the word is reflective of the epistemological framework of the time when the concept was conceived. The framework emphasises scientific, objective and evidence-based knowledge, which has consequences that carry through to its applicability in other contexts. The metaphor of the threshold evokes images of crossing over, into or out of buildings. Liminality, can be alluded to as a doorless passageway from one status to another, the line that distinguishes one phase from another. Essentially, thresholds, and in consequence liminality, bring forward, and reinforce, ideas of lines and structure. Liminality introduces the notion that culture is a production. Understanding culture as a production brings in the examination and analysis to the subjective and situates it within a society or culture. With the actor's point of view becoming central, the focus of research shifts to practice and action, unlocking deeper meanings and understandings (Ortner 1984). With Turner's (1969) notion of performative reflexivity, societies become socially produced, as opposed to a conception of a natural essence of culture. Then, the numerous interactions and interconnections (between categories, structures and also people) appear pivotal. Alongside the production and construction of societies and culture, this epistemological shift creates the possibility for people to reflect, critique and evaluate themselves, and the possibility of changing societal constructions (Wels et al. 2011).

Similar to liminality, the crossroads are perceived as 'betwixt and between' (Turner 1969: 95). However, unlike Turner's concept, crossroads are crossing where multiple choices emerge. The theorisation of crossroads is not modern, they have been studied and analysed through time. They can be both physical (a location) and figurative (situated, or unsituated, in the limbo of space and time). In mythology, the crossroads bridge different worlds. Spirits, deities, ancestors and other supernatural entities tend to congregate in these 'transitional gaps between defined, bounded areas' (Johnston 1991: 217). Rituals are often linked with the experience of these liminal points, helping to navigate within. Indeed, in her studies of Greek and Roman mythologies, Sarah Johnston underlines the 'variety of rituals or superstitions connected with crossroads' (ibid: 217). Gods and spirits help to guide individuals through these spaces and phases of transition, where gifts were left, and altars created. According to Johnson, crossroads can also be conceptualised as places to leave polluted materials banned from society. The liminal nature of these sites, 'liminal point[s] par excellence' (ibid: 220) make them particularly appropriate to get rid of undesirable materials.

Furthermore, the concept of crossroads is not solely embedded in the mythical. Indeed, crossroads are also transitional phases within a social environment, on economic, cultural and/or political standpoints, all three fields being tightly linked together. Characterised by their ambivalence and ambiguity, they can be experienced by an entire community or individually. These contradictory spaces, as epistemological tools, allow us to question our assumptions of human experience and relationships, and even our concept of time. Indeed, through their unsettling nature, crossroads raise questions and challenge established convictions. Thus, crossroads are heuristic tools, offering a fluidity marking the space of social negotiation, with ideas of mobility and hybridity emerging. Being at crossroads implies the idea of potential multiple identities.

Crossroads and borderlands overlap theoretically, but they are metaphorically and genealogically separate. Border studies propose to inform notions of being, becoming and being-becoming in relation to physical borders, such as the one between the United States of America and Mexico. Authors of the movement propose the re-mapping of border zones by embracing their own experience of living in marginalised, interstitial cultural spaces, those zones of resistance to racial, class, gender oppression and discrimination. Indeed, the border, in border consciousness or mestiza consciousness, has come to represent the various immaterial and symbolic spaces of conflict, oppression and discomfort, which Chicana writers inhabit and embody (Akçil 2013). Chicano/a represents a self-chosen identity claimed by some Mexican Americans and emphasises the fluidity and hybridity of their belonging. Therefore, border consciousness, put simply, is the acknowledgement that one exists in a perpetual state of straddling multiple, often incompatible, identities and life-worlds, by existing on the border, with one foot planted on either side (Oliver-Rotger 2003). 'Nepantla' in Nahuatl, an Uto-Aztecan language spoken in Mexico, means 'in the middle'. The term represents these entangled spaces on the borders of competing modes of existence, manifested as either battlegrounds or crossroads of negotiation of the self and the society. These borderlands are described as 'vague and undetermined' places, not only geographically but straddling the various facets of social life (Anzaldúa 1987: 3). Therefore, typical to the metaphors of space in Chicana literature are images of marginalisation, oppression, discomfort and struggle, but also the possibility of overcoming by constructing a mode of being which engages these worlds without conclusively selecting one over the other. Drawing from a plethora of thought-worlds and metaphors, the writings of Anzaldua and Moraga in particular, successfully straddle the dichotomies constructed to constrain and oppress their various identities as *womxn*[1] who do not comfortably identify with the neat categories prescribed by the various racist, sexist and classist structures in which they are, at least partially, embedded. Anzaldúa (1987) conceptualises Mestiza consciousness as a theoretical framework to deconstruct patriarchal and colonialist logics that affect the Chicana psyche. She emphasises the promotion of indigenous spirituality and feminist cultural archetypes. In navigating the dichotomies, drafted through a history of oppositional binaries created by these structures, by claiming ownership of in-betweenness, rather than opposing one binary opposite with another, writers such as Anzaldúa allow for the inherent contradictions within their identities to co-exist within this metaphorical space of negotiation of the self and the community.

Key themes of critique

Metaphors

The key to understand the conceptual shift taken on by the authors of this text lies in our refinement of our understandings of metaphors, and the very real implications they have in ordering our 'realities'. This section, therefore, deals with providing a baseline guide for our theoretical position on the role of language, specifically which of spatial

[1] *Womxn* is a term with a specific theoretical meaning, history, and genealogy. The term originated in 1971 at the University of California. Its conceptualisation has been influenced by Kemberle Crenshaw's work on intersectionality (1991). In South Africa, the term participates in the decolonial discussion of higher education following the protest movements that started in 2015.

metaphors, in shedding light on certain aspects of 'reality' while concealing others.

Metaphors go beyond words by reflecting human thought processes and are, thus, mirrors of our ontological positions (Lakoff and Johnson 2008). Stemming from this, representations of 'truth' are always contingent on forms of understanding and ordering, emanating from particular conceptual systems. Thus, Lakoff and Johnson argue that there is no fully objective, unconditional or absolute truth. Thus, far beyond figures of speech, metaphors serve as 'dominant paradigms. … [that] are transmitted to us through the culture made by those in power' (Anzaldúa 1987: 16). Lakoff and Johnson state that 'our ordinary conceptual system, in terms of which we both think and act, is fundamentally metaphorical in nature' (Lakoff and Johnson 2008: 3).

Therefore, the hegemonic discourses employed in the construction of dominant metaphors in academic literature find their basis in the ontological assumptions, or what the two authors term 'myths', of Western-centric perspectives (ibid: 18). These are the contradictory myth of objectivism and myth of subjectivism. The former entails, among other things, that we understand the objects in our world in terms of categories and concepts which have properties that correspond and interact with the properties of other objects. Thus, in an objective reality, things can be stated to be objectively and unconditionally true or false, and this truth or falsehood can be discovered through scientific methodology. This myth also purports that words have fixed meanings and we can, thus, express precisely the concepts and categories that we think in accordance with. Subsequently, people can be objective and speak objectively, given that the language is clearly defined. To be objective is to be rational, which is perceived to be a good quality as it triumphs over our emotions and biases. On the other hand, the myth of subjectivism purports that most of the day-to-day tasks that we undertake as individuals are reliant on our senses and intuition, which can both be applied to important issues. Therefore, the most important factors for individuals are these subjective feelings and sensibilities relating to aesthetics, morality and spirituality. Subsequently, the language of imagination must be employed in order to express these personal aspects of our existence. Thus, objectivity is perceived as threatening what is significant to individual persons, making science redundant to our internal lives (ibid: 188–189).

These contradictory myths paint the human individual as irrational and sentimental. On the other hand, guided by science, objectivism becomes the universal ordering truth. These form a dialectic, existing as two sides of a coin, contingent on each other for their existence. Each individual understands in which realms of life it is appropriate to operate objectively, and in which realms subjectivity is required in order to act based on the correct cultural codes. Generally, in post-enlightenment Western-centric perspectives, objectivism has taken on a more prominent role in the realms of science, law, governance, morality and so forth. Thus, despite Lakoff and Johnson's argument that objectivism is merely a myth, as the dominant myth in Western-centric perspectives and philosophy, it has gained a hegemonic hold on the way in which our societies have been structured both socially and materially.

Through their work on language, the authors further the discussion criticising the rigid divide between structure and agency, which stems from the Western-centric objectivism that establishes demarcated categorisations between material and immaterial objects. Through Lakoff and Johnson's point of view, the divide, rather than being a reflection of universal truth, can actually be read as a manifestation of specific ontological positions and as such, shed little light on the porosity and pliability of social life.

Therefore, as bounded in specific cultural systems, metaphors such as the threshold, the crossroads and the borderlands offer few possibilities to expand the kinds of 'realities' the authors aim to render visible and the kinds of 'realities' that remain masked in the world of opportunities. Moreover, these have very real implications for the material 'realities' which are constructed based on the binary structures of inside–outside, structure–agency, male–female and many more. That said, despite the constrictive and structuring nature of metaphors, they can also offer vast potential. Because metaphors can restructure the collective conscious in both visual and linguistic ways, the unconscious of those who use them can be altered with alternate metaphorical constructions, making the appropriation and alteration of metaphors a resistive and constructive practice (Aigner-Varoz 2000).

Linearity and direction

The metaphors explored in this text, liminal thresholds, crossroads, borderlands and, thereafter in a subsequent chapter, shadowlands, are all spatial metaphors, stemming from a particularly objective construction of 'reality', which privileges clear boundaries and precisely defined, complete and distinct objects within these defined parameters. Although we could expand the discussion seeking to overcome limited and bounded understandings of these metaphors, the physical limitations of liminality, crossroads and borderlands are the focuses of the chapter. Lakoff and Johnson (2008) argue that it is natural for us to structure language metaphorically around space and time due to the linear order of speech. However, Giddens (1990) traces the conception of the spatial metaphor to the construction of the time-space division following the rise of modernity. Drawing from Thomson (1967), he underlines the emergence of the mechanical clock as a common commodity, as the root cause for the increased awareness of time as a concept to impose order on society. Subsequently, this time-oriented order became related to and imposed upon geographical spaces. Therefore, time came to be understood as constructing and linear, while space took on a bounded, inflexible nature. More recently, however, this hierarchical relationship of time and space has come to be challenged in the social sciences due to the homogeneity of history and experience they produce when employed in this sense (Mohanty 1992). Therefore, the emergence of more fluid metaphors of space and place have allowed for the conceptualisation of alternate forms of temporality, and with that, a multiplicity of subaltern narratives. Moreover, perhaps due to colonial and other histories of spatial marginalisation, the metaphor of space has come to be widely employed in matters of resistance through assertions of claiming or reclaiming spaces from which one has been previously excluded. Following from this, the use of crossroads and borderlands as temporally ambiguous and spatially fluid metaphorical places owes its existence to these developments.

Due to the perceived nature of human bodies as distinct from the environment which we inhabit, despite being hotly debated in the social sciences, we have, in general come to experience the rest of the world as beyond us through a division of inside–outside (Lakoff and Johnson 2008). Thus, we come to perceive ourselves as distinct containers, and seek to see other entities as such as well by endowing them with an orientation. This is true of both man-made objects such as rooms and houses, as well as natural entities, such as rocks. Moreover, in addition to imposing orientations on objects, we also perceive them to have clear, natural boundaries. If a clear boundary is not present, we may seek to impose a physical boundary, such as a wall or a fence, to mark the inside off from the outside. This is obviously related to human territoriality, but specifically to particularly Western-centric notions[2] of the quantification of space (ibid). Therefore, the imagery evoked through these spatial images remains constrained by metaphors of boundaries, as thresholds, crossroads and borders necessitate clear divisions between one space and another in order to describe the movement of the objects that are perceived to be contained in one space or another. This hinders the projected function of crossroads and eventually borderlands in blurring boundaries between structure and agency. Additionally, the linearity of the divisions implicit

---

[2] We could expand the discussion wondering what 'Western-centric' really means, and how ideas of 'the West' are constructed in essentialist ways even by Westerners themselves (the example of *Occidentalism* comes to mind). Indeed, it may be argued that labelling certain modes of thought as 'Western-centric' serves to perpetuate the idea of a dichotomy between 'the West and the rest'. This is especially important in a work that positions itself as critical of binaries and dichotomies.

especially in the metaphorical construction of crossroads also functions to limit the concept.

Victor Turner's (1969) introduction of chaos sparked numerous possibilities for anthropological analysis, but the linearity of the overarching epistemological framework later rendered it a limitation. A constructed dichotomy between structure and chaos – or the unstructured – created opposing poles in existence. The movement between these binaries have been singularised and imagined as unilinear, which is in part due to Turner's perception of a singular society. Implied in this view is that a society is maintained through phases of being and becoming via an individual's, group's, collective's or generation's role in it. Emphasised in this line of thought, a society was made up by roles and identities which functioned to maintain the structure. The transition between these roles was demarcated as liminality, or zones of transitions and unstructured being. Accordingly, the liminal person became 'undifferentiated' due to the notion that 'it' did not have an identity outside the structure (Turner 1969: 96). Additionally, the experience was theorised to occur at the margins of a society. Liminality and society, or being, were two separate spheres with the threshold acting as the doorway in and through to the other.

The imagery conjured up by crossroads is one of lines, suggesting a certain rigidity of movement in a predetermined set of directions and a naturalised dissection of space. Indeed, the quest toward universal standards of measurement that has regulated the crossroads of space and time has enclosed the concept of crossroads in a defined, regulated realm. While originally universal metrics enabled a practical set of tools for colonial rule, they also can be conceived as 'new ways of stabilizing the randomness and chaos produced by the violence of colonialism' (Adams 2016: 20). These universal metrics aiming to organise chaos and incoherence move off the contingent and fluid nature of the crossroads as emphasised in Tutuola's work, especially in his *Palm-Wine Drinkard* (1952). In the piece, different worlds are enmeshed, the protagonists' identities are continuously discarded and recomposed, and boundaries are fluidly overcome, with ideas of lines and separations constantly blurred. Furthermore, the story, the elements composing it, as well as the author, his readers and the world we inhabit are simultaneously shaping crossroads and integrative parts of them. Nevertheless, in an environment dominated by ideas of measurement and linearity, it requires deep considerations to conceive crossroads through their contingency and fluidity. Although the metaphor of crossroads potentially overcomes bounded and linear perspectives, direction and linearity are integrative components of the concept and the specific focus of this very section. Therefore, the idea of crossroads as a spatial point of junction presents the spatial characteristics of boundedness and linearity, potentially limiting the concept. As features of infrastructure, or human constructions, crossroads carry within them the assumption of a governing structure determining their position and direction. Ang (1998) clarifies why the metaphor of the crossroads signals a heightened sense of paradox. The paradox is that, the very self-reiteration of cultural studies is conceived as a transdisciplinary, transnational enterprise, and an intellectual crossroads of people and ideas coming from different locations and encompassing a wide range of focal concerns, approaches and interests. It is a point of contact between multiple ways of being. However, the process of deciding a direction includes a disconnection and the moving away from the point of interaction. Therefore, the idea of crossroads opens up as much as it closes off. On the other hand, the borderlands are theorised to be entirely a space of contact.

While the linearity implicit in crossroads remains rather rigid, Chicana border thought has taken steps to bridge the dichotomies presented by time and space by employing a metaphor of parallel existence. Rather than linear trajectories of movement, the social negotiation in the borderlands occurs betwixt and between the worlds one inhabits. Thus, the linear metaphor functions as a split between simultaneous modes of existence, rather than an indication of movement from one to another. Cherríe Moraga addresses this in 'La Guera' (1997) by describing herself as a woman who refuses the border division, despite straddling it with one foot on either side. Thus, simultaneously inhabiting more than one distinct container functions as a form of refusing the demands of choosing one world over another. This aims to blur and confuse the binaries implicit in existing in or around borders, by allowing for a multiplicity of being, coloured by contradictions and ironies akin to Haraway's cyborg (1991). Thus, the border person, or transgressor, does not simply move away from inhabiting the borderlands, but rather dynamically negotiates his position within the various structures on either side of the border. That said, the linearity implicit in the border metaphor still posits a clear boundary to be traversed and negotiated. The border person remains somewhat constricted to the rigidities implicit in the binaries demanded by the distinction of one world from another, as much as they may wish to murky the border that divides them. Finally, the use of 'borderlands' in the sense that it is considered to bridge the boundaries on either side of the border and create a shared symbolic and physical space functions to mask the different paths taken by its inhabitants to arrive in this space, and thus, works to conceal the various historical and power dynamics within them (Ang 1998).

To conclude, Gupta and Ferguson (1992) point out that imagining spaces as bounded and distinct is a process of naturalising them. Thus, dealing with spaces, physical or symbolic, without unpacking the historical and social dynamics implicit in their construction is a process of masking and perverting the power relations embedded in this terminology. Therefore, in addition to interrogating the formation of communities, societies and feelings of belonging, it is key to question the very spaces in which they have been imagined as contained (Gupta and Ferguson 1992). More fundamentally, it is essential to inquire what kinds of interactions and processes have taken place in the act of depositing one imagined social entity onto another. This naturalisation of physical spaces consequently has a direct impact on the naturalisation and objectification of symbolic spaces. Therefore, the linearity implied in this naturalising process limits the potentialities of interpretation, on physical, but also social, cultural, historic levels. The metaphor of lines presents severe ontological limitations due to the colonial and other histories evoked by spatial imagery. Finally, this bears relevance to discussions of being, as through understanding the process of masking and erasing the implicit in the naturalisation of spaces, we may also begin to unpack the forms of being constructed for and through these spaces.

Being

This section aims to briefly address the forms of being prescribed by the metaphors within liminality, crossroads and borderlands. Therefore, the section interrogates the idea of being in the way it is presented either in the singular or multiple manifestations across these theories, taking into account the repercussions thereof on notions of wholeness or completeness, as well as the ways in which being within these spaces is posited against or within structures. Subsequently, the forms of being postulated in each of these positions is shown to have a bearing on the binary constructions of 'reality' that is particularly prominent in Western-centric thought. Moreover, specifically with reference to crossroads and borderlands, this section argues that the kinds of beings inhabiting these spaces extend beyond the human, across species and 'realities'.

During the liminal phase, the liminal persons undergo a process of deconstructing and reconstructing their social being. 'The "threshold person"' is an ambiguous being, who characteristically possesses nothing, is naked or poorly clad, has no status, property, honorific signs or kinship relations; he or she lacks some of his or her humanity' explains De Pina Cabral (1997: 33). The primary purpose of this phase is to mould the liminal individual or collective for roles in a society that they are marked to enter, which is usually an upward movement through a social hierarchy. Miriam Aurora Hammeren Pedersen (2018) associates her experience as a transgender person in early and middle-stage transition with an intense process of construction, as a car in a garage. Citing her journal, she explains feeling 'like a car at an auto shop. Broken open, tools lying everywhere, rust, dents, etc. visible for all to see, and most importantly: Halfway fixed, halfway broken' (2018: 47). Therefore, embedded in this perspective is the assumption that there is a potential completeness to a being, their personhood and status, which can be achieved by the end of the liminal process. Nevertheless, not every rite leads to a complete being. In male initiation rituals for example, to become a man one must undergo the trial but also father children and care for them, take on age and seniority specific roles, maintain a household, etc. The outcome of an initiation ritual is not always a 'complete being' but a person who is sanctioned to take on specific roles and in so doing to begin the process of becoming a man. Although, in ritual processes, the liminal persons are stripped and left in the liminal space as 'incomplete' persons, the desired outcome is known and the liminal persons are thrust toward it and reconstructed to suit that role or status. Thus, the end goal of the liminal process is to produce, or lay the foundation for the production of a structured, more equipped being that is designed for his new role in a society. This results in a tension between the concept of being and that of becoming, where the structure of a singular being and the process of becoming in the liminal phase are clearly separated. In the first phase of the ritual process, there is a singular being, who progresses into the second, liminal phase, to become a liminal being and is in the process of becoming a new singular being of the third phase (Turner 1969). However, the liminal persons are not considered singular beings until they have achieved the specified social markers that allow them back into a society. The conceptualisation of this singular and potentially complete being contradicts the incompleteness of becoming that does not produce fixed entities but is a continual process.

In the case of crossroads, 'being' appears to be the characteristic of supernatural entities. Magic and daemonic powers found their substance at crossroads, these uncertain places, where spirits and ghosts gather. In Greek mythology, Hekate, and to a lesser extent Hermes, helped to guide individuals through these spaces and phases of transition, where gifts were left and altars created (Johnston 1991). These gods appear as an embodiment of being at crossroads. Moreover, the forest, place of contingence and unknown, where laws and rules are often inverted, is directly linked with the metaphor of crossroads. Thus, animals, species other than human that dwell outside villages, represent beings in these liminal spaces. The crossroads' being is a state beyond binary identity. The Trickster, for example, is a figure of the crossroads. He is described as straddling two worlds: this world of humans and the world of deities. That mythological character has many names and faces in different religions and mythologies, but his role and ambiguity remain a common ground throughout folklore. A figure of mediation, he personifies the plasticity of the natural and supernatural world, which eventually become one, as Tutuola demonstrates in his *Palm-Wine Drinkard* (1952). Neither good, nor bad, nor neutral, the Trickster breaks down order by introducing chaos but, simultaneously, also brings harmony and order to chaos. He, or she, embodies and creates an infinity of possibilities. The mythical personage is simultaneously, in all the worlds of possibility, and between them eluding categorisation. The Trickster, never fully in one place, is a being that opens up the possibility for many realities to intersect. The West African Trickster, Eshu is often portrayed as a man with a limp because his legs are of different lengths, in order have one foot in the realm of the gods and the other in our world (Hormann and Mackenthun 2010: 178). Being becomes a physical experience loaded with emotion and conflict, both torn at crossroads and afraid to stay confined within a unique identity. Past experiences and knowledge are carried by entities (individuals, as well as communities) in these spaces of junctions. The affect is indeed central in crossroads. Being at crossroads conveys the idea of multiplicity of identities, tightly linked with Kemberle Crenshaw (1991) and her concept of intersectionality, the multidimensional situation in which Black *womxn* are embedded. Individuals in crossroads situations are constantly reshaping themselves, facing choices and defining decisions.

Kimberle Crenshaw (1991) criticises the singular narrative of identity and being. She observes that there is an interlocking and multifaceted experience of identity and power. Identity is not a singular experience in that it can co-exist, conflict and cause friction with other identities. These identities are layered within a temporary manifestation of 'reality' and within an actor or actors. Arising from the co-existence and interaction of identities, intersectionality manufactures nuanced and differentiating 'realities' within a temporary manifestation. Crenshaw breaks down the boundaries around identities and makes room for multiple identities and cultural hybridity. Individuals, or actors, are multidimensional beings. This connects with Chicana studies and the notion of borderlands.

Through border thought, the state of being is conceived in relation with hybridity and multiplicity. Also termed 'mestiza' consciousness, it is a 'new value system with images and symbols' that could bridge the divides between 'white [...] and coloured, [...] male and female' and the hegemonically differentiated 'us' and 'them' (Anzaldúa 1987: 3). Thus, being on both the societal and individual level is understood as focused on a holistic entity constructed of various, often contradicting and conflicting parts. Much like Haraway's cyborgs, this form of being at the threshold in border consciousness is construed as a manner in which rigid binaries of male–female, spiritual–physical, life–death, god–human and many more, can be reconciled through a 'fusion of opposites' (Aigner-Varoz 2000). Also described as being a 'crossroads' or a 'battlefield' in this space rife with contradictions, the border persons, rather than conclusively choosing a fixed location, oscillate between positions in a state of suspended liminality – constant in-betweenness (Oliver-Rotger 2003). That said, the form of being dictated by the marginalised position of these border persons and the spaces of internal and external conflict which they straddle, results in a form of being fundamentally marked by a feeling of alienation and discomfort. This is embodied in the writings of Anzaldua and Moraga as a feeling of a split self, of uncomfortable incompleteness. Therefore, the form of being dictated by the borderlands metaphor remains constrained by a quest for wholeness through healing the rupture of the self, or the 'wound' of borderlands (Akçil 2013). Finally, the form of being within borderlands, like at crossroads, extends beyond the material world, due to its nature as dreamlike and imaginative spaces bridging together the worlds of the living and the dead, the human and the non-human and the natural and the supernatural (Oliver-Rotger 2003).

Therefore, it can be argued that the development of the metaphors from liminality to borderlands above indicates a shift toward a more comprehensive and flexible notion of being, allowing for the interaction, and ebb and flow, between previously oppositional binary positions. Rather, the shifting metaphors begin the work of stitching together a web of intersecting and interacting forms of being which account for the essential unfinishedness and multiplicity of being in the world (Nyamnjoh 2017).

Becoming

Crucial to the conceptualisations of liminality, crossroads, borderlands and shadowlands (that we propose to unpack later in the introductory chapter) is the idea that they are spaces for the process of becoming. Becoming in these concepts can take varying forms. It can reproduce the structural hierarchies of a society, but it can also be a space where these hierarchies are challenged by people in that very process. This section tackles how the concepts of liminality, crossroads and borderlands theorise the process of becoming in these spaces, with a particular focus on the manifestations of resistance and marginality as features of becoming, which interact and intertwine to create a change in the structures of a society. The meaning of marginality has changed across time and through societies. The concept is multiple with ideas of spatial, social, economic or ecologic forms of marginality (Gatzweiler and Von Braun 2014). Marginality can be understood as the temporary state of having been put aside, of living in relative isolation, at the edge of a system (cultural, social, politic or economic)

(Kollmair et al. 2005: 10). Inhabiting a marginal space – being excluded – is rarely a matter of choice or deliberate. It is rather a judgmental categorisation for nonconformity to the mainstream philosophy. Resistance can emerge from marginality as the process of defying the hegemonic system, the mainstream philosophy. It has been an important source of inspiration in anthropology, especially during the two last decades of the 20th century. James Scott in *Weapons of the Weak* (1985) connects the idea with dynamism and mobility. Resistance is in constant flux. Furthermore, Scott proposes to understand the concept through its everyday form, overcoming the previous focus on visible and organised mass mobilisation. Overall, the concept of resistance is still highly debated; there is little consensus on its actual definition. Nevertheless, resistance and marginality are closely related.

In liminality, the manifestations of resistance and marginalisation demonstrate how the process of becoming in the liminal space could create a change to the social structure of a society. Liminality grew from its original conception to be a political and economic exclusion on top of it being an emotional, psychological, social and, at times, a geographic isolation. The politics of recognition bonded to the concept imply that the liminal persons are defined by those who are more entitled or more embedded in society, which is possible with the implied 'purity' in being and the attached hierarchy (Turner 1969). These politics also imply that there is a legitimate being that is attained through the achievement of social markers, and if this specific type of being is not achieved, then the individual is considered to still be in the process of becoming and, therefore, still in a liminal phase. That state of 'in-between' is rarely conceived as being a desired process. Failing to achieve the specific type of being sought for is imbued with discrimination and misrecognition. This is particularly emphasised in the notion of waithood. Waithood was conceptualised to explain prolonged period or permanent residence in liminality by individuals or collectives. This containment of personhood is due to the unachievable social markers (Honwana 2014) and is potentially disregarded. Individuals occupying that transitional space are still in a 'waiting' state. Therefore, the liminal beings in waithood inhabit a perpetual state of becoming, challenging the applicability of the concept of liminality in which a singular social status must be reached. Furthermore, the notion of waithood is dynamic. Gender transitioning is a good empirical example of this dynamism. Indeed, in this transition phase, individuals experience a rich and eventful process of construction; the liminal beings do not enter a static state. Therefore, retrieving from Honwana's argument, it would be fallacious to imagine that nothing is going on in waithood (Honwana and De Boeck 2005). Overall, 'other' beings are placed somewhere 'in between', still in a transitional state toward reaching the ultimate goal of being from a particular societal sense, which implies a certain notion or expectation of completeness, wholeness and authenticity of being. Liminality then becomes a zero-sum game, which does not account for the intrinsic variability of social life and the nuanced dynamics implicit in identity formation as a continuous, faceted and incomplete process.

As mentioned above, the liminal persons, in Turner's (1969) conceptualisation of them, are ambiguous, stripped of their social being, and redressed with the social expectations and status of a new being, which designs and orders a society along a hierarchy that is self-sustained. It is in this manner that a societal structure is able to reproduce and in-group identities are preserved. Thus, the theoretical shifts within and regarding to liminality posed resistance, conflict or friction to the maintenance and preservation of a society. It simultaneously opens up 'reality' to manipulation and a non-static experience despite the continuation of a selected reality. Consciousness, choice and decision making became players in social negotiation and liminality. Liminality is no longer a doorless passage through which people transition, but rather it is a transitory space where resistance, conflict and selection reside. The socially designated door for liminal persons to exit is not the only option.

The metaphor of the threshold that is deeply rooted in the concept of liminality suggests an 'outside' or 'between' structure. Thus, the liminal space has been understood as located outside, but on the cusp of a social structure. This eventually correlates with the concept of marginality, although being marginal does not necessarily mean being outside but rather being 'at the edge of a system' (Kollmair et al. 2005), adjacent to, in a less dominant position, as Janice Perlman showed in her study of *favelas* (1976). The liminal space and marginality can be distinguished through two understandings. The first refers to the duration of the adjacent experience. The liminal phase is often a short, temporary state a person travels through, whereas marginality can be, and most often is, a prolonged, permanent state of being. The second understanding, which is not accepted by all theorists, is that the liminal persons usually have a choice whether they undergo the liminal process. On the contrary, marginality is based on the social status of the individual, which is often not designated to them by their choice, and often a direct result of race, sex and/or class. Thomassen (2009) précises that the liminal person is placed on the margin of society, however, it is only momentarily and their reintegration back into their society is expected after the liminal process has ended. The function of the liminal process is to produce members of a society that will uphold their structures and processes, not challenge them (Turner 1969). Thus, liminality perpetuates the structures in place.

At crossroads, entities 'become'. They position themselves in a marginal space, able to visualise a bigger picture and different possibilities of choices. Crossroads open up opportunities to re-invent the self, facing choices for a becoming. In ethnographic fieldwork, people embody the excessive and unruly nature of becoming. Indeed, subjects of ethnography push the boundaries of abstraction through their ambiguous, creative, and unpredictable dispositions. Biehl and Lock make explicit the links between becoming and crossroads stating that 'the time of becoming is the real time in which life struggles are waged, in which stasis is sustained or transformation plays out, fragmented and uneven. It is a time of crossroads' (2017: 10). Hence the responsibility of anthropology 'to think of life in terms of both limits and crossroads – where new intersections of technology, interpersonal relations, desire, and imagination can sometimes, against all odds, propel unexpected futures' (ibid: 318). The authors further argue that becomings create holes in dominant theories and interventions and unleash a vital plurality; being in motion, ambiguous, and contradictory; not reducible to a single narrative; projected into the future; transformed by recognition; and thus, the very fabric of alternative world making. There was a shift in the understanding of becoming in crossroads, which allowed for an unfinished, or incomplete, being. Pushing the discussion further, the Deleuzian perspective, which would presuppose undetermined crossroads, 'gives way to multiple possibilities and makes visible crossroads where choices can be made beyond the shadow of determinism' (Biehl and Lock 2010: 344). Therefore, that suggests a degree of uncertainty and unfinishedness in the crossroads.

In the context of borderlands as a space of social negotiation for people on the peripheries of social structures, becoming can be interpreted as stemming from both resistive activities as well as experiences of marginalisation. These are intimately intertwined in terms of context and action, but the resistive activities relate to the way in which one becomes through challenging the structure, while marginal experiences relate to the manner in which one reconstitutes one's personal experiences of the oppressive structure in the first place. The marginal experience does not automatically imply the process of challenging the structure but rather represents the way the marginalised people compose and navigate within it. While ritual liminality relied on politics of recognition in the reintegration of *persona limina* into the structure, the border person process of being-becoming is specifically shaped by experiences of partial recognition or misrecognition. Oliver-Rotger (2003) suggests that the intertwined web of challenges and conflicts faced by Chicana authors has spawned a form of resistance built on conviviality by accepting a multiplicity of being, for the purpose of constructive social and individual transformation in the face of oppressive structures. Nyamnjoh (2017) reinforces the idea through his understanding of conviviality as a way to promote and preserve incompleteness. The Cameroonian anthropologist, who emphasises notions of mobility and incompleteness in his work, permits to rethink our relationship with completeness, and underlines that 'being human is permanent work-in-progress' (ibid). Stemming from these perspectives, the contradictions within the self and a society cannot be disavowed, but must be embraced for the ironies they produce. Subsequently, the selves that arise from border conscience reflect the way in which 'all people are "subjects-in-process" and that, to the extent that they are constituted by discourses, they are multiple and (to some degree) incoherent' (Moya 2002: 455). This results in a reconstruction of their identity as a form of resistance against the patriarchal, racist and classist structures which they straddle. Through figurative means of reappropriation, reinscription and synthesis of old metaphors, which have formerly functioned to further discriminate, the Chicana authors modify the practical and symbolic implications of the dominant discourse in their favour – and the favour of otherwise marginalised groups (Aigner-Varoz 2000).

The second, deeply interrelated, feature of becoming in border consciousness is that stemming from experiences of marginality. This manifests from the social ostracism experienced by those inhabiting fixed locations on the periphery of multiple oppressive structures. Specifically, those who fail to play their socially ascribed roles and statuses to a satisfactory level (Aigner-Varoz 2000). This existence on the borders is a permanent residence, as despite attempts to assimilate, one cannot fully shake their marginal status as somehow socially incomplete or inept.

Therefore, becoming in borderlands always takes place at the margins, whereby the individual must navigate a space which has previously systematically and violently excluded them (ibid). As such, borderlands are fundamentally a space of discomfort, but also present the possibility for a creative renewal and reconstruction of the self, thus changing one's experiences within an oppressive structure. Therefore, an astute understanding of one's social location in relation to those producing the dominant discourse is fundamental in reconstituting the ways in which one perceives oneself in these structures. Subsequently, interrogating the alternate implications of life on the threshold or border allows for the regeneration of oneself, which in turn holds the potential for challenging the social and symbolic landscapes of the structures (Oliver-Rotger 2003). Thus, becoming is the process whereby the fragmented self – produced by the various oppressive and violent forces at borderlands – becomes reconstituted as a hybrid of contradicting parts, which in turn manifests through the agency of these individuals as a challenge to the hegemonic powers and structures.

Structure and agency

Throughout being and becoming theorisation, notions of agency and structure emerge as separate entities that are mutually exclusive and presented in an oppositional relationship. This carries with it the implication that power is to be understood as residing in these distinct spheres rather than in their entanglements, and therefore, the shape that social negotiation takes is contingent on the nature of these power relations. As Bourdieu (1990) explains, the emergence of these separate entities arises from an objectivism of the social world by stating what is natural and defining the principles in actors' relationships or actor–object relations. In the quest for objectivity, structures emerge as deconstructed and removed from human practices, choice or what would be considered their agency. Structures appear as removed and natural entities dissecting and organising space or species (Bourdieu 1990). Following this critique, the author situates structures rather as calculated and strategic performances that manufacture organisations.

Liminality, as theorised by Turner (1969), was pivotal in the construction and categorisation of structure and agency. Liminality reconceptualises 'culture', thereby situating structures as subjective and imagining an additional and separate space, chaos, which was necessary for structural formation. Turner's predecessors approached culture and society from an objective perspective and undertook an abstract mapping of 'other' cultures (Ortner 1984). Underlying this approach is the assumption of individualised, 'natural' ways of being. This assumption reflects in the theorisation that societies have a social 'base', which determines a superstructure, and from which it draws its formations. People's actions and their societal connections are, therefore, a result of the superstructure rather than the people's actions being fundamental in structure or culture. Turner ruptures this epistemological framework with his introduction of chaos and its interactions with structures (ibid), thereby building the foundation and constructing the separate and problematic categories of structure and agency that are now restricting the conceptualisation of being and becoming. Originally, the concept of liminality was not theorised alongside agency. Turner's (1969) epistemological view might not have included personhood or identities beyond persons' social function. His theoretical shift, on the other hand, allowed for proceeding theorists to introduce agency, willpower and actors. The subsequent introduction of agency alongside Turner's divide and categorisation of structure and anti-structure paved the way for a dichotomous relationship between structure and agency. Anti-structure became the only site for agency to be practised as it has been theoretically framed as being free from structures (Ortner 1984).

As reactions to liminality's linear structure and agency construction, crossroads and borderlands propose to move away from binary constructions. However, the metaphors simply morph, and manifest boundaries, structures and lines in a new form. As such, neither of these concepts detaches itself from the constraints of the structure–agency dichotomy in a satisfactory manner.

There is a sense of masking and naturalising the structures within crossroads. Crossroads hold greater possibilities for agency in a multiplicity of beings, but each being and practice of agency is still bounded to an underlying structure. In conjunction with this masked dictation is the separation between the structure and the actor, in that the actor's agency has no impact on the formation of crossroads, and the structures are pushed as background scenery that misleadingly seems to play no role in the dictation of agency. Therefore, crossroads reformulate liminality's construction of structure and chaos divisions, but do not do away with them. The concept presupposes the existence of institutional structures guiding agency. Institutional structures are comprised of the 'cultural or normative expectations that guide agents' relations with each other' (Elder-Vass 2008: 281). In Williams's conceptualisation (1976), the use of structure at crossroads can refer to different elements. It can, for example, refer to a whole entity that is shaped by the relations between its parts, which shall be called 'structure as a whole'. It is in this sense of structure as a whole that we can conceive of wholes as having powers by virtue of the arrangement of their parts. Regarding crossroads as concrete sites, Chambers (1994) alluded to the fact that we all know that traffic through crossroads is never free-flowing and uncontrolled. Similarly, that there are traffic lights, road signs and rules that all road users must obey, for example, those approaching the crossroads from a minor road are supposed to give way to those passing through from the main road.

In border thought, agency is perceived as something the Chicana feminists construct for themselves, through their literary practices, on the peripheries of oppressive and constrictive structures. Borderlands are productive precisely because the experiences and voices coming together in them 'intermingle with the weight of particular histories that will not fit into the master narrative of a monolithic culture' (Giroux 1992: 209). However, this utopian notion of borderlands as productive, transformative and resistive spaces writes away the historical power dynamics embedded and entangled in them (Habermas 1984). Consequently, the resistive agency developed on the borders or 'margins' are in direct reaction to the hegemonic powers of the centre. Therefore, agency for Chicanas is akin to Scott's *Weapons of the Weak* (1985), whereby they construct subaltern discourses to manifest an existence that, to varying extents, contradicts and subverts the hegemonic discourse disseminated by the accepted structure. That said, despite being on the margins, this agency is still practised within the domain of these structures and is specifically constructed vis-à-vis the dominant discourse with the purpose of altering or challenging it, in order to alter one's experiences and position within it. Therefore, a notion of structure still persists as something to be opposed, presenting a Hegelian problematic whereby the vehement opposition of a structure, at least initially, functions to solidify its legitimacy as something worth opposing. Thus, the negation of a specific structure may function to enforce it in practice, as it acknowledges its power. Accordingly, with Dirlik (1994: 97) the metaphor of borderlands presents the spaces as 'locations of equal cultural exchange', but once one works to unpack the historical power dynamics implicit in the formation of the conceptual tool, one simultaneously unmasks the assumptions of structure and agency fundamental to their theorising.

Unfinished and incomplete

Behind the metaphor and the analytical tool of shadowlands lie the intertwining theories of unfinishedness and incompleteness theorised by Biehl and Lock (2017) and Nyamnjoh (2017). These authors mull over the issue of being and becoming within the existing epistemological paradigms. Becoming, from their observations, troubles and surpasses the knowledge frameworks in place. In Biehl and Lock the act of becoming forces reflexivity and thinking 'against the grain' (2017: x). It leads the anthropologist to consider the unexpected, unprecedented, unknown and uncertain. In order to engage with becoming, the two authors call for an empiricism that has an analytical openness to complexity and imagination. The concept of shadowlands tries to answer this call. The notion grounds itself and thinks through the continuous transformations of 'realities' and being. In addition, the conceptualisation of shadowlands overcomes academic boundaries, examining how being-becoming is understood beyond academia. Within this search, Amos Tutuola's *The Palm-Wine Drinkard and His Dead Palm-Wine Tapster* (1952) was found to have grappled with being-becoming and has become an inspiration for shadowlands.

This idea of incompleteness and borrowing is striking in *The Palm-Wine Drinkard*, in which one of the characters, the complete gentleman, has the capacity to gather different limbs from others in order to ephemerally appear as a complete man. When not borrowing body parts, he is a mere skull. Through this borrowing process, the gentleman gains social recognition and achieves his goal of marriage. A powerful interpretation of the character is that he is at once more than and less than the sum of his parts. The premise of the temporary complete gentleman plunges the subject and being down the rabbit hole of incompleteness. Being is not only fluid, constructed and intersectional, but it is encompassed by unfinishedness, incompleteness, imagination, possibility and mobility. It can be discarded, carried, performed, regressed and regained in the subject. Being and becoming temporarily materialise through a consciousness that attributes its meaning, in that this consciousness holds the ability to enable, disable and vacate components of presence or being. Incompleteness and temporary beings may conjure negative connotations, but in actuality, they aim to highlight the inherent and intangible possibilities within and without.

Moreover, through this, Tutuola (1952) prods us to see beyond the walls of materiality. The subject or things are not inherently complete in their being with moments of liminal incompleteness, but rather inherently incomplete with possibility and momentary manifestations of completeness. The process of becoming and temporary manifestation of being are also not limited to the materiality of a 'reality'. Rather, incompleteness is encompassed by creativity, innovation, aspiration, imagination, potentiality and mobility. This epistemological perspective pushes analysis to potentially see beyond 'reality' to what can be. In relation to this perspective, being transforms into a process of adoption and manifestation according to context, necessity and possibility (Nyamnjoh 2017). Being and becoming in this sense are not bounded by time or place, as the liminal process has prescribed.

Alongside this malleability of being-becoming, unfinishedness incorporates a series of problematics that have emerged in the course of anthropological theory, which includes the human and non-human interactions. It aims to demonstrate how social forms partake and are shaped by multiple systems and forces in which they are themselves contingent and shifting. Becoming demands more than flat realism of contextualisation, determinism and historicism (Biehl and Lock 2017). Beings are not only projected in the present 'real' or the historical 'real', but being is also projected into a multiplicity of possible futures, although materially we only live one of them.

Shadowlands

Metaphors and terminology are living concepts as they are created, used and changed alongside and within experiences. Yet, metaphors and terminology can also be discarded when they can no longer communicate the desired experiences or no longer seem applicable to certain situations, which have been found in the names of prior theories of being-becoming. Liminality, crossroads and borderlands are restricted by their epistemological frameworks, especially with their focus on the 'other', the anomaly, the marginalised, the abnormal. These concepts frame being-becoming within a specific light, location and populace. Each notion is constructed as complete or fixed, which automatically allows for experience to fall through the cracks and leads to a lack of applicability. The conceptualisation of shadowlands has taken this phenomenon into consideration. The concept proposed has purposefully been positioned as incomplete or unfinished to allow for manoeuvrability in its application and reconceptualisation. As a result, the concept of shadowlands intentionally removes the manmade constructions, structures and linearity from the metaphor and rather imbues the metaphor with ambiguity and potential metamorphosis.

Shadowlands is not a new concept or term. It has been a buzzword across popular culture, particularly in dystopian novels, fictional works, comic books and drama. This buzzword has also found itself being loosely applied in academic and scientific works. However, across the various applications of the term, a number of themes emerge. It has been used to denote a 'reality' underneath or within a 'reality'. It is sometimes hidden, intangible and unrecognised. Shadowlands can be a world beyond what we know the world to be, or merely a world beyond what we know. The notion has also been invoked in scientific works around dark matter (Foot 2002). The symbolism of shadowlands and dark matter is an apt one. The observed universe is theorised to only make up a small percentage of the substances in the universe overall. Dark matter, or mirror matter, has been very difficult to concretely observe by the evidence-based methods of the laboratory. Until recently, dark matter stumped the standard laws of science. Scientists have been able to infer its existence only from the gravitational effect it appears to have on normal and visible matter. It has been theorised to make up the majority of substances in the universe and its existence is the only explanation for why the universe operates the way it does. It does not react with light or electromagnetic radiation, but rather only interacts with a gravitational force and gravitationally affects other matter (ibid). Metaphorically, dark matter speaks to similar issues within shadowlands, in that it exists everywhere and within everything, but can hardly be observed outside of its effects on the tangible. This intangibility, shadowiness or darkness does not mean that it is nothing but rather indicates there is more than the observed 'reality'. Furthermore, shadowlands are not only connected to the spatial metaphor. Indeed, they are closely related to time and propose to overcome a bounded understanding of time/space. Shadowlands, by definition, are produced by the play of light and dark. The notion of movement becomes then pivotal; the light is available because of the movement of the earth around the sun. Shadows, therefore, are not fixed, but rather constantly changing through time. The concept of shadowlands derives from this conception and implies an understanding of a moving, mobile time/space.

Shadowlands and their application in popular culture imply that there are multiverses and multiplicity of being. It was by means of novels and fictions that the journey began for the authors in naming and conceptualising the analytical tool as shadowlands. The implausible and the intangible becomes possible with fictional characters and fictional 'realities' coming to life in the everyday (Funke 2003), which fanned the flames of the respective authors' imaginations and presented a multiplicity of potential beings. In the context of drama, shadowlands are a screen on which actors' shadows are cast. All the viewers can see are these fluid silhouettes as the actors' bodies create shapes and morph into other shapes. The actors behind the screen are unidentifiable and the audience fills in the shadow during the transformation between human and object (Pilobolus Dance Theatre 2011). The human then becomes more than and less than what they are. It imposes an ambiguity in species, spaces, times and meaning. Thus, the 'in-between' is not necessarily limited to a human 'reality' and the predictable reaction, continuation, challenge, deconstruction or reassembling of structures, which the liminal passage in liminality made possible. The 'in-between' within shadowlands highlights the multitudes of possibilities that exist at any given point with a thing or subject. The unpicking of concrete boundaries allows for shadowlands to manifest in and across various worlds, such as the spiritual, biological, religious, political, social, technological and economic. In social science, and more specifically anthropology, the concept of shadowlands challenges pre-established and rigid notions and overcomes an anthropocentric vision of the world by acknowledging the connections and interdependencies between worlds. The human is not at the centre anymore. The concept widens the scope of research, and also intends to liberate potential interpretations by incorporating new narratives and following complex dynamics.

Shadowlands: Analytical concept

Tracing the applicability, limitations and conceptualisations of liminality, crossroads and borderlands, has inspired the creation of shadowlands. The concept, through the vehicle of a metaphor, builds an additional epistemological framework. It furthers the potentialities of analysis and contributes to a better understanding of being-becoming. There are two guiding features that lead the epistemological framework of shadowlands. Not separated by rigid frontiers, these two features are intertwined; the dynamics of navigation between them structure the concept. The first speaks to the issue of categorisation, dichotomies and completeness. This feature is theoretically inspired and built upon the notions of unfinishedness and incompleteness. Incompleteness, the constant flux of the 'real' and temporary manifestations, continuously renegotiates the nature of boundaries and frontiers (Nyamnjoh 2017). In some sense, it is the ways these boundaries are navigated, as the Chicana examples suggest. Incompleteness highlights the blurred, mobile, intermingled and porous nature of the frontiers. It is upon this body of theory that shadowlands can situate themselves into being-becoming and state their relevance to understanding the process of being-becoming. The second feature, on the other hand, tries to incorporate a multidimensional gaze in contrast to liminality's singular narrative. It was inspired by the theoretical contributions of Crenshaw's (1991) intersectionality. The aim behind the incorporation of the multidimensional gaze is the integration of a multiplicity of cultural senses and forms of being.

Unfinishedness and incompleteness derail the notion of static completeness, which was previously theorised as complete notions of agency, structure and 'reality'. Incompleteness supplements this construct with temporary and mobile manifestations of completeness, also implying ideas of dynamism and movement. Being becomes a continual process of adoption and manifestation according to particular context, possibility, aspiration and necessity (Nyamnjoh 2017). Primarily, the idea of incompleteness aids in sidestepping polarised dichotomic constructions in previous theory around being and becoming, because it allows one to dwell on complex 'in-between' spaces. It fosters and allows for dimensions and nuances in agency, which were previously constricted and posited in relation to the 'reality' that the liminal persons, transgressor or Trickster experienced. Inspired by incompleteness and unfinishedness the concept of shadowlands incorporates the theoretical perspective to break down the binary between being and becoming, and for shadowlands to manifest as the eternal shadow over being-becoming. Being is never complete or permanent. Nor is becoming a shapeless inventory, absent of being, or a temporary process. Being and becoming are closely intertwined and in a constant push–pull relationship. Through this particular prism, shadowlands represent the never-ending business and site of being-becoming. However, the concept proposed does not mean that there is not a sense of continuation or relative stability between temporary manifestations or being-becoming. Shadowlands give space for the self and selves to continuously and unpredictably experiment with their self-making, with temporary selves appearing in temporary manifestations of 'realities'. Indeed, tightly embedded with the concept of shadowlands is its fluid and malleable nature. Shadowlands are a time/space where possibilities for borrowing, trading, interweaving and a multiplicity of beings are liberated. It requires movement to navigate and negotiate within these spaces. Furthermore, shadowlands are themselves mobile entities, never finished. They are dynamic and in a permanent state of motion and reconstruction. The incompleteness that characterises shadowlands grant them the capacity to constantly renew themselves along with those who reside in them. Bearing in mind Crenshaw's theory of intersectionality, shadowlands theorised that 'being' can exist in a multitude. Thus, being is and can be simultaneous beings. Beings can partially emerge or emerge intertwined. If multiple beings manifest, there need to be degrees of becoming and multiple negotiations of becoming that can communicate with each other. Becoming does not necessarily incorporate the entirety of an actor's being or beings. Rather, these beings can undergo becoming separately, which allows for an actor to be simultaneously being and becoming.

The concept of shadowlands purposefully erodes former categories and conceptualised dichotomies within prior theorisation of being-becoming. The conceptualisation and categories have become restrictive and brushing over multiverses of experience. Shadowlands do not aspire to formlessness, but they rather aspire to resituate the viewer or researcher. The concept makes no claim to be an entirely emancipated space, like liminality's blank slate, or a disciplined space. It intentionally breaks away from the reductionist structure and agency dichotomy. Stemming from this, shadowlands can be seen as spaces allowing for an increased fluidity of power relations due to the break from the rigid, general order of things. This results in a space of multilayered and intertwining forms of power and agency and, therefore, the dissolution of rigid structures and binaries. To cite Michel Foucault, 'Power is everywhere, comes from everywhere', thus it is never possessed entirely through agency or by a structure, but exists in constant state of flux and negotiation (Foucault et al. 1998: 63). The concept of shadowlands is not about being 'for' or 'against' a structure, but rather it is about the site of negotiation of being-becoming with mobility, fluidity, creating, recreation and dissembling the manifestations of power. Therefore, the longevity of structures is an illusion as there are only temporary manifestations of various intermeshed power dynamics, although some of them are durable and have lasting effects. However, the shadowlands concept does not aim to undermine the struggle for recognition and the power dynamics around being-becoming in cases of discrimination, misrepresentation and a lack of recognition. It merely aims to expand on these struggles by the inclusion of imagination, fluidity and complex manifestations of agency or *habitus* rather than the struggle being solely a retaliation to the tangible, static and structural.

This erosion of the category of structure and its dichotomous relationship with agency and anti-structures gives possibilities to social negotiation, formerly understood through the linearity of liminality and boundaries of borderlands, to occur in various localities and within the structure rather than solely at the margins or as a pariah. Aside from sidestepping the restrictiveness of dichotomies and the erasure of experiences, the renegotiation of structure and agency is vital to broaden this analytical tool to encompass being-becoming in the everyday, everywhere and quasi-events. Shadowlands are spaces where being can be discarded, carried, performed, regressed and regained in the subject and temporary manifestations of 'realities' that have a historical, economic, political, linguistic and social situatedness. Shadowlands are simultaneously separate, extending and infused into being and 'reality', similar to a shadow. Being-becoming transforms into an everyday project following into every interaction and 'reality'. It is not limited to special or marginalised expressive spaces, but rather also extends to the taken-for-granted and ordinary mental work, interactions and spaces where being-becoming negotiation takes place. Therefore, shadowlands can be conceptualised as a part and parcel of everyday life, and can appear as seemingly insignificant events or unconscious decisions. The prior conceptualisation of structures overlooks the significance of quasi-events, the embodiment of institutional being responsible for the construction of 'reality', and the social change or negotiation occurring within institutional or societal organisation previously seen as 'structures'. These former 'structures' are not fixed or only open to change by outside agents or outsiders. Thus, agency, structures, and 'reality' take on a new form and conceptualisation. A key contribution of incompleteness, then, is the way in which it creates dimensions to agency and introduces nuances to the formerly rigid dichotomies characterising our ideas of structure and agency.

The guiding feature of incompleteness and unfinishedness used in shadowlands allows for shaking off the shackles of materiality and the tangible by incorporating the intangible. Thus, shadowlands continue to transform the vision of anthropology and widen the scope of research. They exclaim that the business of being-becoming is not exclusively tied to the plausible and the tangible. Rather, it is the intermingling of the tangible and the intangible. Shadowlands are the metaphorical site to represent the phenomenon where subjects or agents through and with their memory, possibility, imagination, social negotiation and 'realities' fraternise, interplay, borrow, create and clash during the constant negotiation of being-becoming. The interactions and blurring between the tangible and the intangible have a direct impact on being-becoming, how being-becoming is understood, and the sense-making within being-becoming.

Liminality opened up the possibility of various ways of sense making with the introduction of the subjective gaze, but shadowlands aim to also incorporate sense making that does not follow the notions of evidence-based logic, rationality and the tangible constructed by the Western-centric framework of knowledge. The idea of shadowlands challenges the dichotomy made between the 'natural' and the spiritual, or the intangible. The notion permits to shift away from the idea that only the empirically confirmed and the logically consistent are the variables that should be considered in analysis. In anthropology, emotions, smell, taste, vision and dreams are now valued and recognised as relevant variables in analysis. The concept proposed considers these variables and proposes to carry on the understanding of these various forms of sense making in research. It contributes to liberate additional or supplementary narratives and permits, at the same time, to understand old ones through different approaches. In this sense, the shadowlands theory is not trying to open up who can enter the space of shadowlands, but how shadowlands are identified, experienced, negotiated and communicated at these points of negotiation.

To sum up, the proposed usage of the concept of shadowlands in this work aims to resolve some of the key limitations of previous theorisation around being-becoming, such as its one-dimensionality, expectations of wholeness, marginalisation, fixedness, unilinear trajectory, focus on dichotomies as well as its oversight of the importance of quasi-events to social life. This book posits that by virtue of its multidimensionality and a focus on the multiplicity of powers, actors and dynamics, shadowlands appear to be a far more nuanced prism through which to inspect processes of social negotiation. Therefore, by acknowledging and embracing the essential incompleteness of human beings, shadowlands allow for far more complex theorising on the dynamics implicit in being-becoming. This extends well beyond the deterministic, linear and dichotomous view of liminality. Finally, the genealogy of the term in both folklore and critical theories has loaded it with sufficient meaning and legitimacy to perform both political and analytical functions. Therefore, shadowlands can be applied to a number of scenarios, phenomena and even quasi-events, dealing with the negotiation or transformation of the individual and a society. Finally, as stressed throughout the work, the concept allows the theorist to extend beyond the constraints of the material world, the human being and society, and imagine a fluid space of interaction between agents, perspectives and worlds.

A brief presentation of the other chapters in the volume

The other chapters in the volume propose to present potential and concrete applications of shadowlands, unveiling eventual criteria for its use.

In Chapter 2, Irinja Vähäkangas, through the prism of the shadowlands, proposes to interrogate the role played by food in the negotiating process of being-becoming. She applies the concept to food and body, unmasking the various power relationships implicated in the process of being-becoming. First focusing on food as a form of shadowlands, then turning to an analysis of the body, Irinja, who draws from Appadurai (1990) presenting the lives of 'things' overreaching the material qualities, underlines the flexibility of boundaries. The shadowlands linked with food and with the body overlap and are inextricably intertwined. Indeed, what is ingested becomes an inseparable part of one's physical being, as transcribed by Conklin (2001) through his analysis of cannibalism practised by the Wari of the Amazon forest. Throughout the discussion, Irinja stresses the character porous of the human body, which represents society in itself; as a site of incorporation of both itself and its cohorts. Various dichotomies are blurred and overcome throughout the chapter, such as the self and the social or the material and the immaterial. Strict conceptions of temporalities and localities are challenged. To conclude, the process of being-becoming is presented as multiple shadows perpetually cast over intertwined bodies. Irinja eventually concludes on a more epistemological note, relating the nature incomplete and dynamic of the ethnography itself, unveiling its characteristic of the shadowlands.

In Chapter 3, Charné Parrott presents the concept of shadowlands as a tool for understanding being-becoming in relation to multispecies studies and supernatural encounters. As contact zones, spaces of clash and friction, shadowlands are sites where multiple ways of being come into contact, not only humans but also other beings and realities. Therefore, shadowlands open up possibilities, moving away from dichotomies, from the Western-centric framework of knowledge and from static classifications. Retrieving from the work of Smith and Dale (1920), Haraway (2008) and Tsing (2015), Charné underlines the permeability of beings and the plasticity of the 'different' worlds. Supernatural and human realms mingle, the unseen becomes legitimate and potentialities of research open up. Uncertainty, ambiguity and unfinishedness lead the field; allowing for a multiplicity of being and becoming. Tutuola (1952) reinforces Charné's argument through his *Palm-Wine Drinkard.* Being and becoming become unfinished processes of continuous negotiations. Challenging anthropocentrism, the author of the chapter drew inspiration from concepts of 'personhood', 'flexible personhood' (Shir-Vertesh 2014) and 'becoming with' (Haraway 2008). Transcending species-specific beings, processes of transformation into animals, practices of becoming other beings and multispecies personhood are at the core of the discussion. In the chapter, Charné aims to underline how being-becoming in shadowlands can assist multispecies studies.

Chapter 4 is an account written by Simone Oosthuizen on the Tunisian uprising. She undertakes an analysis of the impact that electronic media have on being-becoming and how the participation of the Tunisian population, especially the youth, with these electronic mediums had an impact on being-becoming in the revolution. In the Tunisian context, it becomes obvious that the state repression of the possibilities of being-becoming and the lack of civil liberties lead the population to turn to electronic mediums and technological forms of communication. Indeed, electronic mediums provide greater potentialities of multiple beings. They also have the ability to transcend spatiotemporal boundaries, which, in the Tunisian context, permits to overcome state repression or monopolies on being-becoming. By mobilising the notion of shadowlands, Simone underlines the rupture of structure-agency and structure-chaos dichotomies. In the piece, the shadowlands challenge and renegotiate the nature of boundaries, thresholds and frontiers. Notions of imagination, ideoscape and mediascape (Appadurai 1996) are broached throughout the discussion. Simone defends that online social networks facilitate the sharing of imagination, the creation of an imagined community and imagined conviviality, which ultimately brought to the fore new potential and possibility for being-becoming. Alongside this multiplicity of scripts, the sharing of imagination and the resulting imagined communities are constructed across spatiotemporal boundaries. This potential for decentralised and delocalised assemblages implemented by electronic mediums highlight the 'everyday' practice and the quasi-events of the medium.

Simone advocates for the understanding of being-becoming as an overlapping, creolising, interacting multitude, allowing the complex business of being-becoming to co-exist, conflict, interact, influence, appropriate and cause friction.

In Chapter 5, the concluding chapter, Remi Calleja focuses on the various shadowlands emerging within the situation of a postcolonial transition faced by a nation such as the DRC. In that piece, these spaces of junction are considered in their totality, as holistic and dynamic. Not only focusing on their articulation within the various contexts encountered, the author undertakes to highlight the different ways followed by Congolese people and communities to navigate within. Three parts emerge from the argumentation. After an insight into the history of DRC permitting a contextualisation, Remi underlines the physical aspect of the shadowlands. Alongside the concept of mobility that emerges as central and structuring, the place of the body appears pivotal. To continue the discussion, the author emphasises the interdependence of the various social spheres in the specific context, expanding the notion beyond the physical world. Being and becoming within the political sphere, the everyday life and the rites are intertwined and interdependent. Shadowlands frequently manifest from these complex social spaces. Emerging figures and possible responses arising from these situations of chaos constitute the last part of the chapter. Indeed, the shadowlands, in which rules and laws are abrogated, boundaries and dichotomies blurred, become spaces for opportunists and opportunism, including the figure of the Trickster. In that chapter, two main axes lead the epistemological framework of the shadowlands. First, it is the notion of incompleteness, which implies a constant renegotiation of boundaries, a capacity to continually renew itself. Then, the idea of the three-dimensional narrative follows, challenging the notion of unilinearity that is implied by the metaphors of the limiting concepts (liminality, borderlands and crossroads) that the shadowlands propose to overreach.

Conclusion

The concept of shadowlands puts into perspective the business of anthropology and the continuous fabrication of temporalities and being-becoming. An ethnography is a snapshot in time with a focus on the manifestations of and within 'realties'. However, the business is never complete or finished. Maybe the purpose of anthropological work is not to come up with conclusions, but rather to generate sets of questions (Edelstein 2016). Maybe ethnographic work needs to include the malleability and the incompleteness or unfinishedness of 'realities', being, and sense making into the works themselves. To liberate new potentialities of understanding and to contribute to a decolonial thought in line with the actual social context, anthropologists should not only identify shadowlands in their ethnographic research, but also shadowlands in their ethnographic papers that they produce. The concept of shadowlands presents itself even in the continuous figuring out, refiguring and disfiguring of 'realities' and the subjects within the 'realities'. Anthropologists work at both a descriptive and an interpretative level (Biehl and Lock 2017). Therefore, it is necessary to implement an analytical tool to open up the interpretative work to epistemological frameworks of complexity, unfinishedness and incompleteness.

References

Adams, V. (2016) *Metrics: What Counts in Global Health*, Durham: Duke University Press.

Aigner-Varoz, E. (2000) 'Metaphors of a Mestiza Consciousness: Anzaldua's Borderlands/La Frontera', *Melus*, pp. 47–62.

Akçil, G. (2013) 'A Journey into the Depths: the New Mestiza Consciousness in the Life Writings of Cherríe Moraga and Gloria Anzaldúa', Master's thesis, Ankara: Hacettepe University Graduate School of Social Sciences.

Ang, L. (1998) 'Doing Cultural Studies at the Crossroads: Local/Global Negotiations', *European Journal of Cultural Studies*, Vol. 1, No. 1, pp. 13–31.

Anzaldúa, G. (1987) *Borderlands: la Frontera.* San Francisco: Aunt Lute.

Appadurai, A. (ed.) (1988) *The social life of things: Commodities in cultural perspective*, Cambridge University Press.

------(1996) 'Here and now', in A. Appadurai, *Modernity at large: Cultural dimensions of globalization*, Minneapolis and London: University of Minnesota Press, pp. 1–23.

Biehl, J. and Lock, P. (2010) 'Deleuze and the Anthropology of Becoming', *Current Anthropology*, Vol. 51, No. 3, pp. 317–51.

------(2017) *The Anthropology of Becoming.* Durham: Duke University Press.

Bourdieu, P. (1990) *The Logic of Practice*, Palo Alto: Stanford University Press.

Chambers, I. (1994) *Migrancy, Culture, Identity*, London: Routledge.

Conklin, B. A. (2001) *Consuming grief: compassionate cannibalism in an Amazonian society*, Austin: University of Texas Press.

Crenshaw, K. (1991) 'Mapping the Margins: Intersectionality, Identity Politics, and Violence against Women of Color', *Stanford Law Review*, Vol. 43, No. 6, pp. 1241–299.

De Pina-Cabral, J. (1997) 'The Threshold Diffused' *African Studies*, Vol. 56, No. 2, pp. 31–51.

Dirlik, A. (1994) *After the Revolution: Waking to Global Capitalism*, Middletown: Wesleyan University Press.

Elder-Vass, D. (2008) 'Integrating Institutional, Relational, and Embodied Structure: an Emergentist Perspective', *British Journal of Sociology*, Vol. 59, No. 2, pp. 281–99.

Eldstein, D. (2016) 'Allowing for Incompleteness in Research' [Blog], *Princeton Correspondents on Undergraduate Research*, https://pcur.princeton.edu/2016/10/allowing-for-incompleteness-in-research/ (last accessed 17 May 2018).

Foot, R. (2002) *Shadowlands: Quest for Mirror Matter in the Universe*, Irvine: Universal-Publishers.

Foucault, M., Faubion, J.D. and Hurley, R. (1998) *Aesthetics, Method, and Epistemology*, New York: New Press.

Funke, C. (2003) *Inkheart* (A. Bell, Trans.), Frome, UK: Chicken House.

Gatzweiler, F. and Von Braun, J. (2014) *Marginality. Addressing the Nexus of Poverty, Exclusion and Ecology*, Netherlands: Springer.

Giddens, A. (1990) *The Consequences of Modernity*, Hoboken: John Wiley & Sons.

Giroux, H. (1992) *Border Crossings*, New York: Routledge.

Gupta, A. and Ferguson, J. (1992) 'Beyond "Culture": Space, Identity, and the Politics of Difference', *Cultural anthropology*, Vol. *7, No.* 1, pp. 6–23.

Habermas, J. (1984) *The Theory of Communicative Action*, Boston: Beacon Press.

Haraway, D. (1991) 'A Cyborg Manifesto: Science, Technology, and Socialist-Feminism in the Late Twentieth Century', *Simians, Cyborgs and Women: The Reinvention of Nature*, London: Routledge, pp. 149–81.

------(2008) 'Companion species, mis-recognition and queer worlding' in Myra J. Hird and Noreen Giffney (eds), *Queering the Non/Human*, Hampshire: Ashgate Publishing Ltd.

Honwana, A. and De Boeck, F. (2005) *Makers & Breakers: Children & Youth in Postcolonial Africa*, Oxford: James Currey.

Honwana, A. (2014) 'Youth in Transitions and Social Change', in L. De Haan, T. Dietz, D. Foeken and L. Johnson, *Development and Equity: An interdisciplinary Exploration by Ten Scholars from Africa, Asia, and Latin America*, Leiden: Brill, pp. 28–40.

Hormann, R. and Mackenthun, G. (2010) *Human Bondage in the Cultural Contact Zone: Transdisciplinary Perspectives on Slavery and its Discourses*, Münster: Waxmann.

Johnston, S. (1991) 'Crossroads', *Zeitschrift fur Papyrologie und Epigraphik*, No. 88, pp. 217–24.

Kollmair, M., Gurung, G., Hurni, K. and Maselli, D. (2005) 'Mountains: Special Places to Be Protected? An analysis of Worldwide Nature Conservation Efforts in Mountains', *The International Journal of Biodiversity Science and Management*, Vol. 1, No. 4, pp. 181–89.

Lakoff, G. and Johnson, M. (2008) *Metaphors we Live by*, Chicago: University of Chicago Press.

Mohanty, C. (1992) 'Feminist encounters: locating the politics of experience', in M. Barrett and A. Phillips, *Destabilizing Theory: Contemporary Feminist Debates*, Cambridge: Polity Press, pp. 68–86.

Moraga, C. (1997) 'La Guera', *Counterbalance: Gendered Perspectives for Writing and Language*, pp. 269–77.

Moya, P. (2002) *Learning from Experience: Minority Identities, Multicultural Struggles*, Berkeley: University of California Press.

Nyamnjoh, F. (2017) *Drinking from the Cosmic Gourd: How Amos Tutuola Can Change Our Minds*, Bamenda: Langaa RPCIG.

------(2017) 'Incompleteness: Frontier Africa and the Currency of Conviviality', *Journal of Asian and African Studies*, Vol. 52, No. 3, pp. 253–70.

Oliver-Rotger, M. A. (2003) *Battlegrounds and Crossroads: Social and Imaginary Space in Writings by Chicanas*, Amsterdam: Rodopi.

Ortner, S. (1984) 'Theory in Anthropology in the Sixties', *Comparative Studies in Society and History*, Vol. 26, No. 1, pp. 126–66.

Pedersen, M. A. H. (2018) *Crossing the River*, Bamenda: Langaa RPCIG.

Perlman, J. (1976) *The Myth of Marginality: Urban Poverty and Politics in Rio de Janeiro*, Berkeley: University of California Press.

Pilobolus Dance Theatre (2011) *Shadowlands Flower*, SemmelConcertsTV, https://www.youtube.com/watch?v=Z0EO8rhCHhw accessed 24 March 2020.

Scott, J. (1985) *Weapons of the Weak: Everyday Forms of Peasant Resistance*, New Haven: Yale University Press.

Shir-Vertesh, D. (2014) 'Personhood', *The Multispecies Salon*, http://www.multispecies-salon.org/species/ (last accessed 13 April 2018).

Smith, E. W. and Dale, A. M. (1920) *The Ila-speaking peoples of Northern Rhodesia*, London: Macmillan.

Szakolczai, A. (2000) *Reflexive Historical Sociology*, London: Routledge.

Thomson, E. P. (1967) 'Time, Work-Discipline, and Industrial Capitalism', *Past & Present*, No. 38, pp. 56–97.

Thomassen, B. (2009) 'The uses and meanings of liminality', *International Political Anthropology*, Vol. 2, No. 1, pp. 5–28.

Tsing, A. L. (2015) *The Mushroom at the end of the World*, Princeton: Princeton University Press.

Turner, V. (1969) *The Ritual Process: Structure and Antistructure*, London, England: Routlege and Kegan Paul.

Tutuola, A. (1961 [1952]) *The Palm-Wine Drinkard and His Dead Palm-Wine Tapster in the Dead's Town*, London: Faber and Faber.

Van Gennep, A. (1909) 'The Rites of Passage', Chicago: University of Chicago Press.

Wels, H., Waal, K., Spiegel, A. and Kamsteeg, F. (2011) 'Victor Turner and Liminality: an Introduction', *Anthropology Southern Africa*, No. 34, pp. 2–7.

Williams, J. (1976) 'Synaesthetic Adjectives: A Possible Law of Semantic Change', *Language*, No. 52, pp. 461–78.

Chapter 2

Feeding the Shadowlands: Being-becoming through Incorporation

Irinja Vähäkangas

Introduction

In this paper I aim to interrogate the role which food plays in the process of being-becoming as informed by our concept work on the shadowlands. Initially, I wished to take the simpler route of interrogating the ways in which eating practices, especially ones constructed as anomalous, can reveal food to be a shadowland of sorts, which absorbs and masks in it a plethora of meanings and powers. However, when applying this line of argumentation to the ethnographies at hand, the role of the body as a corresponding and overlapping amalgamation of shadows became vividly apparent. Therefore, I have chosen to apply the conceptual metaphor of the shadowlands to both food and the body to negotiate the processes of being-becoming informed by them. Taking into account the nature of the shadowlands as a formation or assemblage (Deleuze and Guattari 1987) of relationships and power-dynamics, predicated on the blurring of boundaries and acceptance of the perpetual incompleteness of the human condition, this paper interrogates the quasi-events and inherent contradictions within these shadowlands. This allows us to extend our scope of analysis by rendering porous the relationships between the individual and the society, the human and the non-human, the material and the immaterial, the 'real' and the imagined and the natural and the supernatural. Therefore, the theoretical assumption this paper takes is in line with Appadurai (1988) in suggesting that the lives of 'things' stretch beyond their material qualities, but also subsume and participate in social relationships.

By weaving together the various narratives and theoretical postulations in the selected ethnographies, I aim to demonstrate the ways in which the shadowlands can be utilised to explore forms of being-becoming which emerge and are negotiated through practices of ingesting and incorporating (Paxon 2016) various substances. I do this as a continuation of the literature which observes the murkiness of the forces of mediating individual identity and social negotiation through an interplay between food and the body. However, I do not propose that these are the only two overlapping shadowlands in the context of the assemblages implicated in incorporation of substances (for instance one could interrogate the role of drugs and medicines etc.), or that the manifestations explored in this paper are the prototype or blueprint for these shadowlands. Rather, I am trying to demonstrate the way in which applying the shadowlands to the concepts of food and the body can continue the work of unmasking the various power relations implicated in processes of being-becoming therein.

I will first introduce the dynamics of perceiving of food as a shadowland, where the shadows cast by social actors, by societies, by histories, economies and politics and communities blend and imbue that which is ingested with specific meanings and powers, which directly play on the process of being-becoming in the context of social negotiation. Thereafter, this paper moves on to discuss the possibility of perceiving of the human body as a shadowland in itself, in the way the individual body and the bodies it is in relations with are in constant and direct interplay with the assemblages of the shadows implicated in materials which are ingested. Consequently, the material body and the meanings attached to it respond and react to the undulation of these shadows, combining, refracting and being absorbed into this space which transcends the self, the social and the material 'realities'. Finally, as this mode of analysis may already indicate, the final section of this paper problematises the treatment of these shadowlands as separate from one another, by analysing the constant interplay between the material and social forces which are ingested and incorporated into one and the other, to argue that it is through the entangled dynamics between these shadow manifestations that the continuous and never complete processes of being-becoming present themselves throughout time and space, transcending all boundaries and defining the incompleteness (Nyamnjoh 2017) which encompasses all existence.

Ethnographies

Throughout this paper, I will be using *Food and Power* (Avieli 2017), *Sistah Vegan* (Harper 2009) and *Consuming Grief* (Conklin 2001) as the cornerstones for analysis. Alongside these, 'Witchcraft, oracles and magic among the Azande' (Evans-Pritchard 1937) and 'Purity and Danger' (Douglas 1966) will function as practical and theoretical backdrops to indicate the continued applicability of more dated ethnographic works as they speak to and across the contemporary works and continue to shed valuable analytical insights.

The first ethnography I will be addressing in this paper is *Food and Power* by Nir Avieli (2017). This culinary multi-site ethnography of Israel inspects various dynamics of social and political transformation through the meanings and processes attached to food and eating and analyses the ambiguous and often contradictory forms of power stemming from these meanings and processes, and how they function to simultaneously cement the cohesion of identity among Israeli Jews and negotiate and reconstitute their power against perceived 'others'. As a contemporary work, the theoretical assumptions of this ethnography in taking on a Foucauldian notion of power-dynamics, of acknowledging locationality as flexible and multilayered, of extending beyond the material and structural implications into questioning the role of the imagination in manifesting certain realities in and through food, this text is particularly pertinent as a cornerstone for inquiring into both projections of shadowlands explored in this paper and functions as a theoretical anchor against which to compare some of the older literature addressed.

The second text used, *Sistah Vegan* (Harper 2009), paints a vivid image of the shared experiences of black females in the United States and those of animals in the animal agriculture industry. The various works collected by Harper address the intersectional identities invoked through dietary choices and their implications on both an individual and societal level. While 'Sistah Vegan' is not an ethnography in the traditional sense, I selected it for the purposes of this paper due to its value in shedding insight on the relationships between the individual body and society and bridging the conceptual gap between humans and animals. By challenging the hegemony of white voices in plant-based eating and animal advocacy, Harper and the other authors address the experiences of oppression experienced by black vegans due to their intersecting raced, gendered and classed identities and situates them in the context of colonialism. Moreover, the selection of this collection of works is a conscious effort on my part to challenge our presuppositions in anthropology of what is legitimised as a form of academic knowledge production. Therefore, the inclusion of *Sistah Vegan* is a deliberate attempt to take steps to defuse West-centric hegemony in my research by questioning the power of academic institutions in marginalising the value of life histories and creative writing in providing important theoretical insights. As such, the use of this work is directly linked to the project of disarming the Western hegemonic power over the means of knowledge production in dictating the appropriate methods for anthropology.

The final contemporary work I have selected is Conklin's *Consuming Grief* (2001), which I predicate the third part of my argument on. In this book, Conklin reflects on the Western Amazonian Wari practices of funerary endocannibalism which persisted as a burial practice until its forced termination by Western powers. She masterfully weaves the various practices of consumption, ingestion and incorporation into the way in which the Wari conceive of their bodies and selves in relation to the bodies which they come into contact with. Through this endeavour, she not only demonstrates the fluidity of human identities and relations, but the ways in which this fluidity and remarkable flexibility of both social and bodily boundaries extend beyond human life into the natural and the supernatural. The thickness of description and the theoretical framework of this beacon of contemporary ethnographic research render the work so applicable for the purposes of this particular paper that it could have, without a stretch, been utilised as the singular source of content. That said, due to the nature of this paper as a comparative analytical work I have chosen to use it primarily in demonstrating the way in which practices of ingestion and incorporation in the Wari context exemplify the interrelated and complex dynamics of the overlapping shadowlands of the consumer and the consumed – the body and the food.

One of the older ethnographies addressed in this paper is *Witchcraft, oracles and magic among the Azande* (Evans-Pritchard 1937). In his classic ethnographic work, Evans-Pritchard argues that the manner in which the various constraints surrounding the way the Zande individual conducts their life is directly related to the ways in which the Azande society maintains and mediates the relationships within it. While certainly dated, the analysis of restrictions on what is deemed acceptable for ingestion, by whom, and when, can provide novel insights once one looks beyond the structuralism implicit in the text, and inspects these dynamics through the ways in which they can shed light on the relations between taboo and power.

Finally, in her benchmark ethnography, Douglas (1966) beautifully addresses the ways in which 'purity' and 'pollution' are contextually constructed and extend beyond the functional, and can be used to analyse the ways in which individuals and societies relate to each other. This makes it an apt framework to draw from analytically in our discussions of dynamics of transformation, of challenging notions of structures and margins, as well as completeness. Thus, demonstrating the analytical value of retrospectively applying the key dynamics of the shadowlands. Therefore, rather than predicate an entire section of my argument on it, I have chosen to briefly address it at one or two relevant points throughout my argument to demonstrate the value of the parallel reading of texts for the contextualisation of concept work.

Food as a shadowland

Robin Fox writes the following on the immense social value of food:

> Food is almost always shared; people eat together; mealtimes are events when the whole family or settlement or village comes together. Food is also an occasion for sharing, for distributing and giving, for the expression of altruism, whether from parents to children, children to in-laws, or anyone to visitors and strangers. Food is the most important thing a mother gives a child; it is the substance of her own body, and in most parts of the world mother's milk is still the only safe food for infants. Thus, food becomes not just a symbol of, but the reality of, love and security. (2003, p. 1)

This led me to imagine the dinner table as a shadowland, a place of interaction, negotiation, of momentarily putting life aside, while doing the very thing that perpetuates this life (Fox 2003). The space in which one dines is one of love, kinship and harbouring commonality, but also a place characterised by a very real threat of conflict when the substances consumed are not physically or symbolically appropriate, and when the actors present are at odds with each other or social norms and customs. That said, not all settings in which food is consumed are spaces of active social negotiation, either in the constructive or destructive sense, but they always hold such potential for both the self and the society. Avieli argues that food embodies the site of channelling social transformations, as a social space where fluid power relations are continuously being challenged (2017, p. 10). Beyond the abstract, food has very real geopolitical implications. The most obvious political manifestation of the norms of inclusion and exclusion are borders, where the specific food items which are controlled, prohibited, imported and exported highlight the nuanced forms of entanglements of power at political meeting points (Anderson 2014). Moreover, nutrition has played a key role in the creation of historical political relations, with implications that still manifest today. For instance, the spice routes were a significant force in encouraging the exploration and appropriation of new territories and galvanised the emergence of new economic networks (Munro 2009).

In *Food and Power* Avieli explores the so-called 'hummus wars' in which the origin of the definitive dish for both Israeli Jews and Arab cultures in the Middle East manifested as a contest to produce the largest serving of hummus (Avieli 2017). He characterises Abu Gosh, the site where Israeli Jewish efforts in the hummus wars took place, as a symbolic space as the 'bridge for peace in the Middle East' (2017, p. 5), due to the multicultural nature of the village and its significance as a site for negotiations between various world leaders. However, he also critiques the ironies of this feat, as the hummus used for the record-winning bowl of the treat was industrially produced and putrid by the time it was served. Thus, he argues that the masking of the contested origins of the dish and its manifestation in this event was a reflection on the political relations in the regions 'foul, putrid, and unappetizing"' (2017, p. 6). Moreover, the culinary culture of Israeli Jews consuming and claiming ownership of hummus in their day-to-day lives, also manifests as quasi-events of claiming power over their neighbours through their constructed culinary heritage, while simultaneously manufacturing internal cohesion through the assertion of a common identity across the ethnic and racial divides which frame the identity of Israeli Jews. Therefore, Avieli argues that despite the contradictions and global as well as regional dynamics reflected onto the dish, this case illustrates the centrality of cuisine to nation building for one imagined community, while posing a direct threat to another. These ironies and contradictions exemplify the way in which various shadows, both material and immaterial, are absorbed and naturalised in bowls of hummus, whether they are utilised as an outright expression of political bravado, a symbol of peace, or a means of harbouring unity of a family or a nation.

Similar dynamics of these parallel processes of construction and destruction can be observed in the application of the shadowlands to plant-based diets in the *Sistah Vegan* (Harper 2009), in which the various life narratives of the authors combine simultaneously to build a sense of commonality between black vegan women and challenge Western hegemony. This conscious construction of a community occurs through the weaving of various alternate discourses, especially Afro-centric ideologies, with specific sets of eating practices. Therefore, by employing alternate forms of knowledge production and epistemological perspectives, these women transform what is often perceived as simply a diet, into a manifestation of a specific ontology and identity. In this sense, food is employed as a tool for integrating people who would not otherwise necessarily come into contact with each other, thus generating positive social change. Moreover, dietary choices in this work are also construed as a means of collapsing the binary between humans and animals by seeking to speak across experiences on either side of the divide and establish commonality based on suffering and oppression. These methods of self-identification also carry within them a purposeful act of political resistance by challenging 'whiteness as the norm' for plant-based eating, by addressing the fallacies implicit in the presumption that veganism stems solely from a Western (white) ethical paradigm. Additionally, by subverting the hegemonic narrative within veganism the authors of this volume are creating a space for themselves within the vegan community, while also addressing the ills of society at large by challenging the systematic deterioration of black bodies as a remnant of colonial domination. Therefore, through simultaneously constructing a community for themselves while aiming to disarm oppressive social forces, the contradicting and intertwining shadows cast by the 'sistah' vegans can be seen as both threatening and filled with potential.

The dynamics above, of construction and destruction, can be further elaborated on by interrogating them through Mary Douglas's notions of purity and danger (1966). Douglas defines 'dirt' as something which is out of place, something which represents disorder. This is exactly what the authors of *Sistah vegan* consider their current position in society to be: under multiple forms of oppression. In claiming ownership of eating practices considered anomalous within their own communities, while challenging the hegemony of white voices in veganism, the 'sistahs' are challenging their identification as out-of-place and less-than. In opposing the norms of social order, these women are therefore reconfiguring both their own notions of purity and morality, while challenging hegemonic ones. That said, while Douglas believed that identifying sources of purity and pollution also functioned as identifying structures, the Foucauldian notion of power adopted in the shadowlands suggests that identifying and challenging ideas of pollution rather functions to trace the conflicting and intermingling shadows cast through various forms in which power is exercised, suppressed, subverted and transformed in society (1998). However, the thesis 'where there is dirt, there is system' (Douglas 1966, p. 36), also suggests that once the binary constructions typical of West-centric thinking are challenged by asserting a multiplicity of identity (vegan, black, female – all at once!), the category of 'pollution' also begins to disintegrate. Therefore, by recognising forms of identification and authority claimed through culinary practices, one may begin to employ tactics akin to Scott's weapons of the weak by challenging the accepted normative order through the subversion of hegemonic narratives (1985).

To conclude, the exaggeration of qualities or meanings applied to food items and culinary practices, reflects the exaggerations implicit in the processes of the creation of normative categories inherent to othering. Therefore, claiming tradition and purity for oneself, while simultaneously labelling the practices of others as unusual, strange or polluting functions to construct and perpetuate the binary opposites of the self and the other. By attempting to identify the various shadows that combine to create these dichotomies, along with their contradicting dynamics and entanglements of power, allows for us to begin the work of uncovering the meanings which they function to obscure, while rendering these binaries a social construct. This has very real implications on our notions of the processes of being-becoming, as the shadowlands highlight the complexities of powers which entangle to galvanise changes in both the self and the society, and allows for a framework of imagining social change beyond significant transformative events by directing our gaze to the quasi-events of continuous daily manifestations of power relations through food.

The body as a shadowland

Recognising the centrality of the body as the site of incorporation for substances consumed, both nutritional and other, this paper now shifts its focus to exploring the possibility of the body as a manifestation of the shadowlands: as the site in which processes of the self and the social intermingle and transform modes of being.

In Evans-Pritchard's *Witchcraft, oracles and magic* (1937), one is presented with the ways in which the simultaneous negotiation of the self and society are inscribed onto bodily practices through the contextual control of what is deemed ingestible, and what is considered socially polluting. Like in Douglas's work, the body becomes the site in which both pollution and social production and reproduction are located. This is exemplified in his discussion of the taboo as follows:

> Men whose habits are dirty, such as those who defecate in the gardens of others and urinate in public, or who eat without washing their hands, and eat bad foods like tortoise, toad, and house-rat, are the kind of people who might well bewitch others ... not everyone who displays these unpleasant traits is necessarily regarded as a witch, but it is these sentiments and modes of behaviour which make people suspicious of witchcraft, so that Azande know that those who display them have the desire to bewitch, even if they do not possess the power to do so (1937, p. 52).

As such, behaviours deemed impure or polluting are attributed to the very materiality of the being of these individuals, as they may be suspected of possessing the 'witchcraft substance' in their bodies, a substance of a reddish colour, containing seeds of pumpkins, sesame and other edible plants taken by a witch from their neighbours (1937, p. 2). Therefore, the witch's body is considered to physically incorporate and embody forces perceived to be destructive to society. The witch is not only dangerous through intent and practice, but also poses a physical manifestation of this threat that can sometimes be observed through the breach of various taboos. Moreover, also an individual who is not a witch, but breaches various food-related, behavioural and sexual taboos may pose a considerable threat to social-mediating practices such as healing and conflict resolution through oracles (1937, p. 52). Thus, following assigned protocol with relation to the way in which one relates to one's own body also reflects directly on the social body. As such, social negotiation is also directly linked to the negotiation of the self and the mediation of the individual body against the other bodies it exists with. Moreover, imagining the body as a shadowland in the context of the Azande allows us to take their experiences of the relationships between the observed social world and the supernatural very seriously indeed. Therefore, examining the entanglement of forces, both social and mystic, allows for us to transcend the material world in analysis and observe the very real implications this has on becoming, on both an individual and social level.

On the other hand, in *Food and Power* Avieli provides a vignette of the perceived relationship between meat, power and masculinity in an Israeli military prison (2017, p. 146). He illustrates the way in which the ingestion of meat is constructed as a means of claiming and subverting power. He demonstrates how the Israeli Jewish soldiers guarding the prison asserted that the lack of meat in their diet in comparison with the Palestinian prisoners resulted in a reversed power dynamic whereby they considered their prisoners to have a comparative advantage over them. Subsequently, this embodied perception of weakness was used to justify acts of institutional and personal abuse toward the prisoners. Thus, the interaction of the shadows cast by dietary practices, personal relationships and socio-political dynamics was considered to intertwine within the physical bodies of the actors in the context of the prison, subsequently negotiating their interactions and power dynamics with each other. Therefore, the bodies of the prison guards and the prisoners became shadowlands which transcended both time and space by incorporating manifestations of historical and geopolitical forces into the physical bodies interacting in the locality of the prison.

Similar dynamics are also observed in a reading of *Sistah Vegan* (Harper 2009), in which the plant-based diet adopted by these women through various personal motivations also imprints on their material bodies. Therefore, the shadows cast on and by society and on the individual self, are also cast on the body which physically ingests this ideology. This is discussed by Harper as a conscious means of decolonising the black female body, thus rendering these women embodiments of their efforts of self-transformation and resistance. In this sense, the 'sistah' vegans are utilising their dietary practices, along with other bodily and spiritual techniques, to physically transform their bodies to oppose institutionalised racism and neo-colonialism. By addressing the colonial residues of 'Soul Food', along with other forms of nutritional oppression felt specifically by black Americans, by virtue of their racial identity and social location, the writers indicate the manner in which the food we eat can also be shown to eat away at us: our vitality, our health and our sense of self in both a physical and social capacity. Thus, the process of going vegan is a process of reasserting oneself against the colonial and post-colonial other by unmasking the intertwining ideologies of speciecism and racism, and changing the way in which one allows oneself to be composed at the cellular level. As Lloyd-Paige writes in *Sistah vegan*:

> January 2005 marked the beginning of my understanding of how food affects the functioning of my body. It was November 2005 that marked the beginning of my understanding of how the food I ate contributed to social

> inequalities, and it marked my transformation to eating like a vegan; in late November I began thinking and eating at the same time. *(2009, p. 16)*

This act of 'thinking and eating at the same time' reflects an awareness of the way in which social structures are incorporated into the body. Therefore, I argue that veganism can be read as an assemblage of the socio-political shadows cast onto the individual body and the conscious processes of bodily conditioning, through both nutrition and ideology, can be seen to cast an equally powerful shadow back on society. Consequently, a vegan can be seen not only to ingest and digest certain types of political and economic agendas, but also incorporate and embody them in a material sense.

Therefore, through these examples we observe that the human body can be interpreted as a shadowland which holds within it parallel, but sometimes contradicting, meanings and powers which interact with the shadowlands of dietary practices. As such, the continuous acts of meaning making around bodily and dietary practices manifest as events and quasi-events which unfold to galvanise, transform and negotiate processes of being-becoming, which transcend the individual, the local, the present and the 'real'.

Discussion

Through the argumentation above on both food and the body as shadowlands of sorts, it becomes clear that the boundaries between the consumer and the consumed are flexible, blurred and context dependent. Even when forcibly separated, it is in fact incredibly difficult if not outright impossible to distinguish that which is consumed from the entity which consumes it. Thus, the shadowlands of food and the body can be shown to be fundamentally overlapping and inextricably intertwined due to the ways in which they each subsume, reproduce and sometimes challenge, both materially and symbolically, assemblages of relationships and sociohistorical dynamics between all manner of things, humans, animals, ideologies, supernatural beings and so on. Therefore, treating the body and the food that it ingests as entirely separate would not only be a detrimental disservice to the proposed concept of the shadowlands, but also the ultimate reductionism.

The ideas explored throughout this paper touch heavily on notions of embodiment (Csordas 1990) in anthropology, as well as Bourdieu's concept of the 'habitus' (1990) as a set of bodily practices, which bridges and problematises the boundary between the individual body and social bodies. Avieli (2017) argues that the foods people eat and the contexts in which this food is produced, disseminated and consumed are 'among the clearest expressions of the habitus'. Therefore, the notion of incorporation becomes central to our analysis (Paxon 2016). It is quite literally the acknowledgement that what is ingested becomes an inseparable part of one's physical being. Douglas (1966) also speaks to the ways in which that which is ingested becomes a part of the body, blurring the boundaries which distinguish it from its environment, arguing that this ambiguity may pose a threat to order. I agree that this transgression of the erasure of bodily margins can hold destructive power for both the self and the social, but I also believe that analysing it through the metaphor of the shadowlands allows us to also examine its productive power in refining our analytical focus beyond the binaries of the self and the social, as prescribed by the binaries previously applied to the boundaries of things in relation to the human body as strictly inside or outside.

Frost (2018) elaborates on these insights, when she writes on how the human body, from a biological point of view, is porous and devoid of rigid boundaries. Thus, what is ingested goes well beyond the food that is eaten and incorporated into the body, one's mental states, relationships, minute instances of contact and interaction with things and beings. These can be interpreted as shadows of historical and social dynamics rendering the body a shadowland, where the self and the social become entangled, where the material and the immaterial meet, where the 'real' and the imagined intertwine, and where the present cannot satisfactorily be separated from the various manifestations of the past and the future. What the 'body' presents itself as now, is an accumulation and an assemblage of various social and material relations, but also holds within it the imprint for various future potentialities that may or may not actualise, depending on the trajectory these relations take. Through demonstrating the porosity of the individual body and the way in which it interacts with its social and material environments, Frost (2018) shows that none of these can be considered truly separate from one another, even within a biomedical paradigm. This can help us also understand the vast implications of the way in which food we ingest becomes incorporated into our very being, thus, beyond being a mere symbolic incorporation of social norms and structures, these norms and structures become part of the very biochemical matter that we are constructed of. In other words, while one may identify some of the individual shadows cast and make estimations on their forms and the various surfaces onto which they are reflected, the blurriness of their boundaries and the unpredictability of the ways in which light directs and conducts them onto these surfaces yield them fundamentally indistinguishable from one another.

While these dynamics of the intertwined shadowlands of the incorporating, embodied body can be identified in all of the ethnographies analysed for this paper, the most literal representation of such manifestations stems from Conklin's *Consuming Grief* (2001). My initial presumption was that the endocannibalism depicted in the work would function as a means of reincorporating the body of a beloved individual into one's own, and possibly by extension the body social, drawing very clear parallels between acts of incorporation and intercourse. Based on salacious tales of Western instances of cannibalism, including serial killers such as Jeffrey Dahmer who wished to keep his victims close for as long as possible, this assumption was soon turned on its head as I began reading. Conklin interprets the 'compassionate cannibalism' among the Wari as being part of a process perceived to transform the deceased body into something entirely unfamiliar before disintegrating and disposing of it through ingestion. Although it may sound extreme or violent, this was done for the deceased to be able to detach themselves temporarily from this life and take their transformative journey into the underwater afterlife. Meanwhile, their kin and community members would be able to relinquish themselves of the pain of the loss by removing any and all physical reminders of their loved one who had passed. The reintegration and incorporation of the dead individual, therefore, did not occur through the consumption following their death. Rather, Conklin suggested that the Wari believed that the deceased individual would return as a white-nosed peccary, a type of wild hog, to offer themselves as nourishment to their close kin, and to, once again, be consumed with respect, love and compassion. It was only in this second act of perceived cannibalism that the person was seen to be incorporated into the embodied bodies of their community members as an accepted source of nutrition. Therefore, in the acts of funerary cannibalism among the Wari, Conklin observed a dynamic whereby the boundaries between those who consume and those who are consumed was inextricably intertwined, rendering the human and non-human actors as fundamentally indistinguishable from each other. As such, it can be argued that the bodies of the Wari, analysed in the context of shadowlands, were an enmeshment of the shadow formation of food and of the body, the boundaries of which oscillated, sometimes unpredictably, to dictate the manner in which the process of continuous personal and social transformation, becoming, was perceived to take place.

Beyond the obvious points of fascination in the ethnography, what also struck me as particularly pertinent was the pivotal role of the incorporation of non-food substances into the body through quasi-events and daily rituals. It was these repeated actions and interactions which played the greatest role in the process of being-becoming among the Wari, rather that the dramatic events of funerary cannibalism. The individual body was deliberately constructed through the repeated exchange of bodily fluids between an infant and both its parents, facilitating the life force of the individual. This set of daily practices was considered to begin at conception and continue through to birth, after which the continued use of bodily practices between the individual and the people they came into contact with would persist to transform the individual's body, in which the self was located, and the body social. These interactions ranged from mundane acts of touching and showing care, to momentous events such as the first act of intercourse, and continuously ushered the individual along their path of being-becoming- from childhood through adulthood and beyond the death of the embodied body. Therefore, these constant actions and their embodied reactions mediated the continuous and never complete parallel processes of individual and social transformation. This was due to the Wari notion of human bodies as porous and relational, rather than bounded by the margins of the individual body, allowing for the physical incorporation of the physical matter of all bodies existing together. Viewing the body in this sense, as a physical manifestation of the entanglement of its social relations, encompassing interactions of the past, present and potential future, resulted in a considerably more fluid notion of kinship and ethnicity. Following the exchange and incorporation of the life substance of significant others into one's bloodstream, an individual was constructed as related to the other by blood in the literal sense, whether this exchange occurred at conception or not. Thus, the identity of the Wari, both individually and in relation to others, was subject to constant transformation and renegotiation.

The incorporating, embodied body is shown in Conklin's ground-breaking work to be the site in which one's past and present kin physically manifest as one. Where historical dynamics are negotiated, and social processes and identities are fused. The transformation of the self throughout one's life cycle through birth and beyond death, is entirely enmeshed with those of their kin who preceded them, and those who are to follow. The individual body is, therefore, physically identifiable as separate from the social body, but in practice one and the same: a body that feels and heals the same wounds, and is perpetually in the process of making and re-making using the same substance. This resulted in a remarkably fluid notion of kinship and ethnicity, but also humanity. The body of the individual Wari was constructed as irrevocably intertwined with the natural environment which it inhabited. Moreover, these beliefs reframed the relationship between humans and non-humans (animals and supernatural beings) as non-oppositional, but rather negotiable through practices of consumption and incorporation. Therefore, the intertwining dynamics of the shadows reflected on the consumer and that which is consumed, in Conklin's ethnography, paint a vivid image of ever-transforming shadowlands, which function to complicate and problematise West-centric binary notions of the body, the relationship between the individual and society, the cultural and the natural, and of 'reality' and myth.

Conclusion

Through examining the dynamics of incorporation and how it can problematise our understandings of the human body as distinct and fixed, one is directed once again to address notions of completeness. Douglas suggests that the human body functions as a metaphor for society in the following passage:

> The body is a complex structure. The functions of its different parts and their relation afford a source of symbols for other complex structures. We cannot possibly interpret rituals concerning excreta, breast milk, saliva and the rest unless we are prepared to see in the body a symbol of society, and to see the powers and dangers credited to social structure reproduced in small on the human body. (1966, pp. 115–116)

However, I believe that this argument can be catapulted further, given the shadowlands analysis of the relationships between the individual and social bodies, to indicate that in its porosity and fluidity the human body *is* in a very real sense society itself: a site of incorporation of for both itself and its cohorts. Thus, by problematising the margins of the human body as socially constructed through a specific epistemological point of view, we are simultaneously challenging the assumed notions of structure and marginality within this epistemology. Following this train of thought, the shadowlands prove to be a fascinating tool for interrogating the way in which temporalities, localities and life cycles intricately fold into each other through the assemblages of relationships and meanings, cast like shadows on the body and reflected back onto the bodies and things it comes into contact with.

Therefore, in this analysis, the shadowlands afford us a vastly more complex notion of the constant intertwining processes of being-becoming, which take place in the various interacting bodies, a process which does not necessitate an end point of static 'being' and is, as such, fundamentally incomplete. This suggests a considerable break in the hegemonic epistemology within anthropology to this day, as being has often been construed as the end goal of processes of becoming through the negotiation of the self and society, creating a dynamic whereby these liminal stages have been considered to represent disorder and social pollution (Douglas 1966). Thus, there lies immense power in suggesting that human existence, in all its ironies and contradictions, is not predicated on becoming complete but simply revelling in the inherent incompleteness of continuous becoming. Therefore, being-becoming is never a clear-cut event to be analysed in its contextual manifestation, but rather various shadows cast perpetually over the intertwining bodies of members of a society and the material and immaterial objects they are in relationships with. As the light shifts over the various shadows, they are redirected, reconstituted, absorbed and reflected in a continuous process of events, quasi-events and practices. Moreover, these are processes that do not occur simply at 'the margins', as boundaries (material, immaterial, social, geographical, bodily and so on) are ambiguous and flexible. Rather, these perpetual processes weave themselves tightly into the fabric of everyday life and between various oscillating dynamics, not simply through the unitary relationship between structures and agents. Just as power can be found and utilised everywhere, the processes of being-becoming also occur in momentary, but constant manifestations throughout the complex, interfolding and cyclical lives of the individual and the society.

To conclude, the application of shadowlands retrospectively on ethnographies indicates that ethnography as a practice is fundamentally incomplete in that it can only ever provide a vignette, a specific point of view and analysis. Moreover, an ethnography is also always unfinished, as it remains open to interpretations and reformulations and, through that, exists not as a historical text, but a living document in interaction with the ways in which knowledge production itself is constantly renewing and transforming. Therefore, the implication for future ethnographic work is not to move away from attempting to provide the most comprehensive treatment of the topic at hand, but accepting that what emerges will not, and should not, be treated as the definitive text on its context. Rather, it will thrive and evolve as it interacts across and beyond anthropological literature. Thus, just as the rest of humanity, it can be argued that anthropologists themselves are also, in fact, intimately and inextricably immersed in the business of unfinishedness.

References

Anderson, E. N. (2014) *Everyone eats: understanding food and culture*, New York: NYU Press.

Appadurai, A. (ed.) (1988) *The social life of things: Commodities in cultural perspective*, Cambridge University Press.

Avieli, N. (2017) *Food and Power: A Culinary Ethnography of Israel* (Vol. 67), Berkeley, University of California Press.

Bourdieu, P. (1990) *The logic of practice*, Redwood City: Stanford University Press.

Conklin, B. A. (2001) *Consuming grief: compassionate cannibalism in an Amazonian society*, Ausrin: University of Texas Press.

Csordas, T. J. (1990) 'Embodiment as a Paradigm for Anthropology', *Ethos*, Vol. 18, No. 1, pp.5–47.

Deleuze, G. and Guattari, F. (1987) 'A thousand plateaus', (Trans. Brian Massumi) Minneapolis: The University of Minnesota Press.

Douglas, M. (2003 [1966]) *Purity and danger: An analysis of concepts of pollution and taboo*, London: Routledge.

Evans-Pritchard, E. E. (1937) *Witchcraft, oracles and magic among the Azande* (Vol. 12), London: Oxford.

Foucault, M., Faubion, J. D. and Hurley, R. (1998) *Aesthetics, method, and epistemology* (Vol. 2), New York: New Press.

Fox, R. (2003) 'Food and eating: an anthropological perspective', *Social Issues Research Centre*, pp.1–21.

Frost, S. (2018) 'Ten Theses on the Subject of Biology and Politics: Conceptual, Methodological, and Biopolitical Considerations', in *The Palgrave Handbook of Biology and Society*, London: Palgrave Macmillan, pp. 897–923.

Harper, A. B. (ed.) (2009) *Sistah vegan: Black female vegans speak on food, identity, health, and society*, Lantern Books.

Munro, J. H. (2009) *Out of the East: Spices and the Medieval Imagination*, New Haven: Yale University Press.

Nyamnjoh, F. B. (2017) 'Incompleteness: Frontier Africa and the currency of conviviality', *Journal of Asian and African Studies*, Vol. 52, No. 3, pp. 253–70.

Paxon, H. (2016) 'Rethinking Food and its Eaters: Opening the Black Boxes of Safety and Nutrition', in Jakob A. Klein and James L. Watson (eds) *The Handbook of Food and Anthropology*, New York: Bloomsbury, pp.268-288.

Scott, J. C. (1985) *Weapons of the Weak: Everyday Forms of Peasant Resistance*, New Haven: Yale University Press.

Chapter 3

Multispecies Encounters in Shadowlands

Charné Parrott

Situating the concept of shadowlands

Mythologies, folklore and fictional literature are rich in the imagery of ambiguous spaces that lie 'betwixt and between' (Turner 1969: 95) the seen and the unseen. The names of these spaces (if it is even ascribed one) and the understanding of who resides within these spaces varies drastically. However, it is clear that they are spaces of encounter and interaction in which humans, animals, plants, monsters, creatures and deities can come together. It is a space of social negotiations; a space of being, becoming and being-becoming. In this chapter, the space will be referred to as 'shadowlands' and it proposes that the concept of shadowlands can be a tool for understanding multispecies and supernatural encounters, and how they can shape being-becoming.

Shadowlands are contact zones for encounters among and between 'beings'. 'Contact zones' is defined as 'social spaces where cultures meet, clash, and grapple with each other, often in contexts of highly asymmetrical relations of power, such as colonialism, slavery, or their aftermaths as they are lived out in many parts of the world today' (Pratt 1991: 34). The purpose of defining shadowlands as contact zones is to illustrate the friction, or clash, that occurs in the space where multiple ways of being come into contact.

However, as mentioned before, shadowlands are not only spaces for multi-cultural interactions among humans, but also other beings and 'realities' entirely.

For the purpose of this chapter, when 'beings' is used it refers to human, animal, microbial, plant and paranormal beings. This word was consciously chosen for two particular reasons. The first reason is that the notion of shadowlands is a movement away from dichotomies that are perpetuated through language. Other scholars, before me and many after me, will also encounter this problem of creating the sense of the 'other' when using terms such as 'humans' and 'non-humans' or 'inhumans', 'natural' and 'supernatural' and 'normal' and 'paranormal'.

Secondly, 'beings' complements the notions of continuous being-becoming and instances where being-becoming take a form that might be considered 'supernatural'. Before deciding on 'beings', 'entities' and 'living things' were also considered. 'Entities' and 'living things' brought forward other issues. Specifically, 'entity' gave the impression of a fixed structure, although it does include inanimate objects, which being does not necessarily imply. However, 'being' as a fluid and unfinished or incomplete concept, and in conjunction with shadowlands, allows for the possibility of a 'reality' in which inanimate objects can be a state, or part, of being. On the contrary, 'living things' restricts 'being' to the world of the living, which does not include inanimate objects or the dead. Shadowlands open up the possibility of a 'reality' in which being dead is a state of being. In *The palm-wine drinkard and his dead palm-wine tapster in the Dead's Town* (Tutuola 1952), the mere skull of the skull people is considered a living being, that can talk, move and borrow limbs to resemble a 'complete' being.

Continuing on this notion of the multiplicity of being, shadowlands allow for 'realities' where animals have 'personhood' and humans can temporarily change into animals. The concept is consciously defined by the authors in a manner which leaves the concept open for further possibilities and imagination. Thus, the shadowlands are imbued with uncertainty and ambiguity. It is a space where boundaries blur and things can become more than and less than what they were before, which allows for being and becoming to be a continuous 'unfinishedness' (Biehl and Locke 2017), 'incomplete' (Nyamnjoh 2017) process, thus allowing for an incomplete being. The concept of shadowlands is an attempt to move away from binaries and dichotomies.

Crucial to the understanding of the concept of shadowlands is that although it is understood as a place, shadowlands transcend physical space and time. It is also not singular – multiple beings can experience one shadowland, or one being can experience multiple shadowlands, as both major events and/or quasi-events. This paper also goes further by suggesting that a being can also be shadowlands for other beings or things.

Ethnographies

The five ethnographies that were used to engage with multispecies encounters in shadowlands were chosen from various discourses and thought eras. The reasoning behind selecting work from various discourses was the manner in which the concept of shadowlands was constructed. Not only was the concept pulled together from inspiration from sources outside of anthropology, such as science journals, drama and fiction, but it also reflects the dynamic interaction of discourse within shadowlands. Thus, of the five 'ethnographies', the first is a short story of supernatural beings and encounters, the second is an ethnography of a particular culture in a particular time and setting, the third and fourth are collections of essays that blur together anthropology, supernatural and science, and the fifth is an ethnography that spans across species, cultures and countries.

The first 'ethnography' is Amos Tutuola's *The palm-wine drinkard and his dead palm-wine tapster in the Dead's Town* (1952), which is a short story that follows a man, the palm-wine drinkard, who searches for his palm-wine tapster through mysterious towns and encountering an array of humans and supernatural beings. It is a story where the 'supernatural is quite simply natural' (Nyamnjoh 2017: 5). This book was chosen because it was the original inspiration for the concept of shadowlands. Tutuola's world is a shadowland for the intermingling of the supernatural and 'natural'. It is a world of endless possibility and uncertainty.

The second is Edwin William Smith and Andrew Murray Dale's *The Ila-speaking peoples of Northern Rhodesia* (1920). This is a thick description of the cultural practices, societal structures and beliefs and understanding of the world held by the Ba-ila, in what is now Zambia. Although the ethnography was written from a very Western-centric perspective, the descriptions of the 'folklore' or 'tales' that the Ba-ila told of supernatural encounters and their ideas about animals and the world demonstrate how contact zones, such as shadowlands, create possibilities for alternative 'realities' and ways of understanding the world in which the distinction between humans and other beings can be blurred or even erased.

Similarly, the third ethnography also advocates for the possibility of other 'realities' or 'truths', other than that of the dominant, Western-centric, evidence-based knowledge. As mentioned above, *Anthropology and cryptozoology: exploring encounters with mysterious creatures* (2016), edited by Samantha Hurn, is a collection of essays and ethnographies of encounters with beings that are unseen or do not fall within dominant, scientific classifications. Cryptozoology is the 'scientific study of hidden animals, i.e., of still unknown animal forms about which only testimonial and circumstantial evidence is available, or material evidence considered insufficient by some!' (Hurn 2016: 1). What should be emphasised here is that this ethnography argues that testimonial evidence should be considered as a form of legitimate 'truth', as anthropology as a discipline has come to value. Thus, this ethnography is relevant for the accounts of human encounters with other beings, and how 'personhood' and the categorisation of beings can be relooked at, and expanded.

Noreen Giffney and Myra J. Hird's *Queering the Non/Human* (2008) is the fourth ethnography, which is also a collection of essays that aim to disrupt current, dominant thinking of the world in order to introduce other ways of knowing and thinking. Similarly, they go a step further by being written to purposely disrupt the notion of what is 'human' or 'personhood'. It advocates thinking 'with' instead of thinking 'of' animals, which opens us to a whole different way of understanding the world. This might not be a new perspective, but it makes it possible for alternative ways of knowing, thinking and being to be as legitimate as the current, dominant, scientific-based understanding. By disrupting the Western-centric notion of the human, this ethnography becomes a shadowland for the interaction and intermingling of classifications of beings, opening up the possibility for hybridity of beings.

The final ethnography is Anna Tsing's *The Mushroom at the end of the World* (2015). This ethnography centres around the life of the matsutake mushroom and all of the other beings it encounters on its journey from the Oregon forest in the United States of America, to the markets of Japan. Tsing's ethnography is a reminder of the impact that human actions have on other beings and the environment, but it also opens our eyes to the unseen world of the mushroom and its connectedness with trees, and the labour, exchange and social structure of humans. In Tsing's work, the beings all become actors within the precarious shadowlands she depicts, but they can also become shadowlands themselves as beings blur and interact within them.

The concept of shadowlands offers a different lens with which one can engage with issues of multispecies and supernatural encounters, and how they can shape the being, becoming and being-becoming of these beings. These ethnographies all offer some insight into the interactions between beings, but they also allude to the blurring of thresholds and boundaries, which are artificially designed. This is integral to shadowlands in which dichotomies and binaries are smudged to allow for a spectrum of experience and 'realities'.

Species

Smith and Dale (1920) introduce the structure of the Ba-ila classification system for animals and plants. They distinguish between *banyama* (quadrupeds), *bapuka* (creeping things and reptiles), *tupuka* (insects), *bazune* (birds), and *inswi* (fish) (Smith and Dale 1920: 224). They then also have a subcategory for *banyama*, which includes, *obadi nfumba* (hoofed-animals), and *bachele* (soft-footed animals) (Smith and Dale 1920: 224). Similarly, within the classification of *bapuka*, are snakes which according to the anthropologists they would classify 'fabulous' (Smith and Dale, 1920: 229). This illustrates how the Ba-ila also added their 'supernatural' beings to their taxonomy, which is logical, seeing as there have been multiple sightings, and they are described in detail to the anthropologists. For instance, the *ikonkola* is a snake said to be 'two hundred yards long, which leaps over trees' and is a 'red and black mixed' colour (Smith and Dale 1920: 229). Although the anthropologists make it clear that this comprehension of the world is not one they would call 'reality', the Ba-ila remind us that the science-based taxonomy, which is dominant in Western-centric education, is not universal, nor is the logic behind it. Similarly, the inclusion of the 'supernatural' snakes is not something to be scoffed at, if one considers that the Komodo dragon (with its 'fabulous' name) had not long ago been understood to have been a mystical creature of legend (Hurn 2016).

If we were to blur the Western-centric, science-based understanding of the human, animal, microbial, plant and supernatural, could there be a possibility of a reality in which there are degrees to 'being' human or animal? As many scholars before have determined, the Western-centric taxonomy of beings has a very specific system for the classification of 'species', but they also argue that it is a system designed by and for the human, as a way of ordering the world (Haraway 2008; Hartigan 2014). The design behind dominant taxonomy is one of 'radical difference', often that which can be observed, but also difference that is logical and classificatory (Haraway 2008: xxv). Haraway's perspective on the classification of species is that of marking the differences of beings, however, species also mark periods of stability in the evolution of being. This suggests that taxonomy is a snapshot of a brief moment 'as organisms transition from one discernible reproducible form to another' (Hartigan 2014).

Although these perspectives allow for the continuous change of specific beings, the classification as a species suggests that beings are fixed to one defined state of being until there is a drastic change in their biology, which would slot them into the next fixed state of being. Shadowlands allow for the multiplicity of being, which suggests that the being-becoming is an unfinished process in which there is a continuous negotiation of forming and deconstructing being as people interact with other beings and things. Thus, in shadowlands, species can fall away as beings become malleable and take on characteristics of other beings, or even fully change into them.

In Tutuola's (1952) short story, his protagonist has the ability, with the help from *juju*, to turn into any animal. In one instance, to prove to an 'old man' that he is the 'Father of gods who could do everything in this world', the protagonist turned himself 'into a very big bird and flew back to the roof of the old man's home' (Tutuola 1952: 7). This ability to transform one's being across species, is also reflected in Smith and Dale's (1920) representation of the Ba-ila's comprehension of their relationships with other beings.

The Ba-ila tell stories of how 'powerful medicine' turns people into other creatures, such as lions, hyenas and wild dogs. These animal-people then slip out into the night to hunt and, at times, to drag 'people out of their huts into the forest and eat them' (Smith and Dale 1920: 125). These stories also allude to the fact that these humans can mutate their being through the ingestion of 'powerful', 'magical' substances. Do these beings then jump from one fixed species to another? Or can being be a fluid, malleable state of continuous becoming, in which the classification of living beings is left unfixed and overlapping? Moreover, what of the question of reincarnation and possession? Do these suggest that a being is simultaneously multiple species at once? The question of reincarnation and possession will be grappled with further under the heading 'Being-Becoming'. For now, it is posed to illustrate the constraints of the classification of 'being'.

Another critique of the dominant taxonomy of beings is selectiveness of the studies of the beings of this world. Our world has barely been studied and systematically classified, and yet new species are being discovered, some have evolved and other become extinct on almost a daily basis. There is a selective interest that different cultures have in certain beings over others. Hartigan (2014) argues that larger carnivores that are encountered more commonly, roam or occupy larger areas and are more 'charismatic' than those smaller and more omnivorous are more likely to be studied in depth. Thus, he states that in Western cultures (particularly of the United states of

America), bears will be more commonly investigated than the skunk will be (Hartigan 2014). This world is vast and shadowlands are opening up our understanding of 'realities' in which the unseen is as legitimate as the impact it has on those who experience it are.

Similarly, micro-organisms, and other small beings hidden from the eye, such as underground mushrooms, were previously unseen but still experienced by beings. The current emphasis on the study of these beings not only opens up the possibility for the legitimacy of the 'supernatural' but also the fluidity of movement across the static categories of species and beings. Microbial beings, such as bacteria, are difficult to situate in the dominant classificatory system because of their reproduction (Haraway 2008; Hartigan 2014). The lateral gene transfer of some bacteria causes tension with the criterion of being able to reproductively interbreed within the same biological species (Haraway 2008: xxv).

Similarly, the question of how a new species comes into being is complicated when the broad spectrum of beings is included. The general theory is that a new species is created by branching off from the original species through a genetic mutation that is drastic enough (and reproduced in following generations) to change a major feature of the species. However, this does not take into consideration 'symbiosis between species, resulting in the acquisition and transferal of genomes' (Hartigan 2014). Thus, if we look at the symbiotic relationship between the matsutake mushroom and the pine trees, with which a 'woodwide web' formed by the mushrooms on the roots of the trees that interlock together connecting entire forests as one and exchanging matter back and forth. There is an exchange of biology when species meet symbiotically. Tsing discusses this further by stating that through symbiosis, 'interspecies relations draw evolution back into history because they depend on the contingencies of encounter' (2015: 142). Thus, the development of a new species can be caused by the encounter with another species. This then brings into question whether this interconnectedness of species still classifies them as wholly different species? Are they not simultaneously two separate beings and one whole being?

Being-becoming

When critiquing the structure of a knowledge tool, one should also consider who created the tool and for what purpose. The human is almost always placed as an outsider to science. The purpose of the concept of shadowlands is to also remove the anthropocentricism from our understandings of being-becoming. The question, 'can thought go on without the human?' is one posed by the editors, Giffney and Hird, of *Queering the Non/Human* (2008). By bringing forward this question it not only guides us towards exploring the capabilities of other beings and acknowledging their cognitive abilities, it also reveals how arrogant humans are to not have acknowledged the capabilities of other beings before. Shadowlands are spacse where the impact that humans have on animals can be revealed, but also where the impact that animals have on humans can be investigated.

If we look at Tsing's *The Mushroom at the end of the World* (2015), the forests of Oregon become shadowlands as multiple different beings congregate at a certain time of the year, matsutake mushroom season. The mushrooms and pine trees, as was discussed above, are already in shadowlands together as their symbiotic encounter creates a oneness of their being, one that is continuously changing as new information (and biological matter) is exchanged between them. Then, enters the human. The humans are mostly made up of informal, seasonal workers who move into the forests to form a shadowlands community, where cultures clash and grapple with each other, but it is still a community of mushroom pickers, buyers and sellers (Tsing 2015). The collection of humans into the forest introduces a disturbance. As one of Tsing's participants states 'if you want matsutake [...] you must have pine, and if you want pine, you must have human disturbance' (2015: 151). This human disturbance is part of the production of the forest; it revitalises the beings encountered. Thus, Tsing's ethnography illustrates how being-becoming is shaped by the encounters with other beings, and how an aspect of one's being can be shaped by something like fungi.

An attempt to bridge the division between the human and 'non-human' is the concept of 'personhood' or 'flexible personhood'. Personhood can be understood as 'the ability to be with others and to form connections with them, whether human or not' (Shir-Vertesh 2014). This connectedness, in Shir-Vertesh's case, is in relation to the accepted amount of human personhood that humans will ascribe to certain animals, for instance, the household pet. The pet is an example of flexible personhood, which is a fluid, continuously changing perception of what can be considered a pet and to some degree as part of the family. This concept brings in the possibility for the relationship between humans and animals to resemble social relationships between humans (Shir-Vertesh 2014).

Therefore, humans can consider themselves as more than just 'owners' of the pets, but also companions, friends, siblings or parents. However, humans also have the convenience of being able to focus again on their 'non-humanness' to justify any exclusion at any stage (Shir-Vertesh 2014).

Haraway (2008) also engages with this idea, but she discussed it rather in terms of 'becoming with'. She argues that humans and other beings are so interconnected that becoming will always entail contact zones, where interactions and negotiations of the self and the other, which construct being-becoming. In conjunction with Haraway's 'becoming with', Wright (2014) suggests the opposite of Shir-Vertesh's personhood, which suggests that humans can come to see through the perspectives of other beings. She states, 'becomings are a form of worlding which open up the frames of what registers to us and so what matters to us (in part by recognizing what matters to others)' (Wright 2014). This suggests expanding the human focus to include the subjective worlds of other beings, for instance 'becoming-dog', entails the observing and experiencing the world 'through encounter with a new relational context', the world of the dog (Wright 2014).

This process is also called 'perspectival multinaturalism' (Hurn 2016), which allows beings to transcend their species-specific being to a form of personhood that is characteristic of other species and as such a human can have lion personhood, or a lion with human personhood. The question here is then how do these beings transcend their own being to take on the personhood of another.

The Ba-ila also dabble in the transcendence of being through the ingestion of certain materials. In the context of personhood, the Ba-ila people can choose to become an animal (or the *itoshi monster*) by taking the appropriate medicine, such as small pieces of hide of the animal they want to turn into, soaking them in water and adding specific roots, putting the concoction aside for it to be infested with worms and then feeding those worms to the individual (Smith and Dale 1920: 125). By ingesting these worms filled with the essence of the animals chosen, the individual can live as a human made up of multiple other beings, with characteristics of those beings. However, the person is only understood to become the beings ingested after death (Smith and Dale 1920).

Kohn (2007) encountered similar practices in his studies of the Runa people of the Amazon. The Runa, much like the Ba-ila, ingest substances to take on the characteristics of other beings. For instance, the Runa smoke bezoar stones because they are considered to be 'the source of a deer's awareness of predators' (Kohn 2007: 6). Hunters believe that if they smoke the bezoar stone, they will encounter more deer. Moreover, some Runa ingest 'jaguar bile to become were-jaguars' (Kohn 2007: 6). Once were-jaguars, the individuals are empowered in their daily lives, however, and corresponding to the Ba-ila, the Runa become jaguars only after they have died (Kohn 2007). The ingestion of the animal substances as a process of becoming that animal, makes the body a space in which the fixed boundaries of species and specific, individual kinds of beings, are blurred and what was once the hide of a lion or the bile of a jaguar, is now the becoming of a different being that is neither human nor lion or jaguar but both. Thus, the body becomes its own shadowland of being-becoming, where tensions between beings come together as one, complex, unfinished being with borrowed parts.

It is important to note that in these practices of becoming other beings, the person does not possess the body of an animal that already exists; instead the creatures are created from the substances that are ingested. In the case of the Ba-ila, they believe that the person becomes the beings chosen after death, but through the development of the worms that had been ingested before death (Smith and Dale 1920). Their bodies are still in the graves in which they were buried, but they are also the beings chosen and their 'spirits' can be reincarnated as other persons (Smith and Dale 1920). Thus, the original person can, after death, be in three places at once, at least (depending on how many beings were chosen). This illustrates how the shadowlands can allow for a multiplicity of being, where so many other beings reside inside one being, and after death this one being could then become so many different beings simultaneously.

The Ba-ila interpret certain interactions with other beings, specifically acts of giving by 'dangerous' beings, as the reincarnation of a deceased member of their clans acknowledging their kin through gifting. Smith and Dale (1920) give the example of a person encountering a feeding lion. If the lion leaves its prey behind after being disturbed, the person will 'recognise' the lion as their deceased friend and thank it for remembering them and leaving them the animal as a gift (Smith and Dale 1920: 128). However, as stated before, the spirit of the deceased is still able to become reincarnated in another human body. The complexity of being-becoming, in Ba-ila ways of understanding their experiences of the world, reflects the complexity of shadowlands that allow for beings to be incomplete and simultaneously more than and less than they appear to be.

Conclusion

The concept of shadowlands enriches the study of multispecies encounters and creates a space in which the supernatural and the natural live side-by-side. The shadowlands blur the man-made classifications and binaries that dominate Western-centric thought, and bring forward a complex understanding of the fluidity of beings in shadowlands, allowing for beings that are incomplete and multispecies personhood. In this paper the terminology was carefully chosen to avoid recreating dichotomies between beings and being-becoming. Similarly, the system of taxonomy relooked at to suggest that there is more than one way of understanding and experiencing the world interacting beings. Lastly, being-becoming in the context of the ethnographies was explored to get an understanding of how being-becoming in shadowlands can assist multispecies studies. By applying the concept of shadowlands to multispecies encounters, it opens up the possibility for beings to be made up of multiple other beings and for their being-becoming to be in constant motion as the worlds of different being impact each other.

References

Biehl, J. and Lock, P. (2017) *The Anthropology of Becoming*, Durham: Duke University Press.

Giffney, N. and Hird, M. J. (2008) *Queering the Non/Human*, Hampshire: Ashgate Publishing Ltd.

Haraway, D. (2008) 'Companion species, mis-recognition and queer worlding' in Myra J. Hird and Noreen Giffney (eds), *Queering the Non/Human*, Hampshire: Ashgate Publishing Ltd.

Hartigan, J. (2014) 'Species', *The Multispecies Salon*, http://www.multispecies-salon.org/species/ (last accessed 13 April 2018).

Hurn, S. (2016) *Anthropology and cryptozoology: exploring encounters with mysterious creatures*, New York: Routledge.

Kohn, E. (2007) 'How dogs dream: Amazonian natures and the politics of transspecies engagement.' *American Ethnologist* Vol. 34, No. 1, pp. 3–24.

Nyamnjoh, F. B. (2017) 'Incompleteness: Frontier Africa and the currency of conviviality', *Journal of Asian and African Studies*, Vol. 52, No. 3, pp. 253–70.

Pratt, M. L. (1991) 'Arts of the Contact Zone', *Profession*, Modern Language Association, pp. 33–40.

Shir-Vertesh, D. (2014) 'Personhood', *The Multispecies Salon*, http://www.multispecies-salon.org/species/ (last accessed 13 April 2018).

Smith, E. W. and Dale, A. M. (1920) *The Ila-speaking peoples of Northern Rhodesia*, London: Macmillan.

Tsing, A. L. (2015) *The Mushroom at the end of the World*, Princeton: Princeton University Press.

Turner, V. (1969) *The ritual process: structure and antistructure*, London, England: Routledge and Kegan Paul.

Tutuola, A. (1961 [1952]) *The Palm-Wine Drinkard and his Dead Palm-Wine Tapster in the Dead's Town*, London: Faber and Faber.

Wright, K. (2014) 'Becomings', *The Multispecies Salon*, http://www.multispecies-salon.org/species/ (last accessed 13 April 2018).

Chapter 4

Shadowlands and Social Media in Revolution: The Impact of Electronic Mediums on Being-becoming

Simone Oosthuizen

Introducing Tunisia and electronic mediums

The world became aware of the growing uprising in Tunisia with the endless tweets, posts, YouTube videos and blogs of mass mobilisation against the Ben Ali regime circulating the internet and online social networking sites, despite a deafening silence of the Tunisian media outlets. The straw had finally broken the camel's back with the self-immolation of Mohamed Bouazizi. Mohamed stood on the steps of the governmental office in Sidi Bouazid, Tunisia, and doused his body in flammable liquid. Whether it was a political statement or a demonstration out of sheer desperation, he brought a light to the liquid and turned his burning flesh into a symbol for mobilisation (Honwana 2013). With his fruit and vegetable stall confiscated by the police officer, Mohamed was pushed out of the last economic sector available for him, like many other youths, attempting to attain financial security in the informal economy (Honwana 2013).

Contextually, the state's repression, particularly political repression, and lack of civil liberties played a significant role in the turn to and the prominence of electronic mediums and technological forms of communication. In 1987, Ben

Ali rose into power alongside promises of greater openness in the political arena and the encouragement of freedom of expression, but the opposite became true after being voted into power (Honwana 2013). Instead of acting on his promises, Ben Ali implemented more repressive measures in regard to the political arena, human rights, civil liberties, mediascapes and ideoscapes than his predecessors. He closed down the political space and targeted other political parties. Civil society organisations were denied registration that allowed them to legally operate or have means to operate. Public meetings, where the state, human rights and political dissent could be discussed, were banned (Honwana 2013). Essentially Ben Ali and the state clamped down on the physical or material means for openness, expression, communication, imagination and being-becoming, which created a dictatorship, or monopoly, in the nation state. Ben Ali used the political, economic and military means at his disposal to initiate and implement the clampdown and monopoly across political spaces, mediascapes and ideoscapes. This monopoly was then maintained by restricting any critique, thoughts and being-becoming that challenged or diverted from the frameworks the monopoly instilled. The restrictions manifested in denied or ignored permits and legal registration, which can be seen in the applications for operations by civil society organisation and thereafter protesters that had to apply for the state's approval to protest (Honwana 2013). The restrictions continued to manifest with targeting, monitoring, harassing and, in some cases, imprisonment of opposition parties, activists, journalists or any individual who spoke out against the state (Honwana 2013).

The state's repression also translated over into economic endeavours, where successful companies that were not owned by Ben Ali's network and competitors to the businesses owned by Ben Ali's network were stifled. In addition, any entrepreneurial activities were not financed and were harassed by the police (Honwana 2013). It becomes apparent across the various manifestations of repression by the Tunisian dictatorship that forms of being, which did not align with the state's vision of being, and attempts to negotiate with being were restricted, stifled and punished. The Tunisian state was able to implement this repression across physical, material, economic and political assemblages of being-becoming and temporary manifestations in a geographically demarcated space. The heavy hand of the state caused the Tunisian populace to seek alternative means of communication and expression, or implement a greater usage of existing means of communication, that the state could not control or repress. There was a turn towards electronic mediums for alternative means of communication and expression, which was influenced by the state's inability to completely control or repress the medium. The state attempted to censor particular video sharing and social networking platforms, which merely led the medium's users to alternative sites or to use proxies to browse censored platforms (Honwana 2013). As a result, electronic mediums, such as the internet with its various platforms, and technological forms of communication, saw a high rate of consumption amongst the Tunisian populace, particularly the youth, in the search for freedom from the state's restrictions on being-becoming. The allegiance and participation with electronic mediums and online social networks exponentially grew in that one in five Tunisian people were noted as Facebook users at the time of the revolution (Honwana 2013). The purpose of this essay is to investigate the impact electronic mediums have on being-becoming and how the participation of the Tunisian population with these electronic mediums had an impact on being-becoming in the Tunisian revolution. The aim of this investigation is to illustrate how the resulting information reveals the complexities within being-becoming. The essay will use the Tunisian revolution in 2011 as an entry point.

The ethnographic snapshot of the Tunisian revolution mobilises the notion of the shadowlands with the rupturing of structure agency and structure–chaos dichotomies. Frontiers, borders and thresholds that appear in anthropological theory around becoming, as mentioned in the introductory chapter, place an emphasis on dichotomies, divides and boundaries. With the intention of expanding previous theorisation around being and becoming, the shadowlands throw 'reality' into a continual flux. Thereby the shadowlands critique and renegotiate the nature of boundaries, thresholds and frontiers. The shadowlands use incompleteness and unfinishedness to resituate and destabilise being-becoming, but the shadowlands also utilise the theory of assemblages to understand, critique and renegotiate the nature and the conceptualisation of boundaries. Incompleteness and the theory of assemblages thrust a spotlight onto the varying nature of boundaries. It can highlight the blurring, movement, intermingling and porous nature of these boundaries. Thus, the incomplete, fluid and temporary assemblage becomes more significant than the boundaries that demarcate them.

Mobilising the imagination and convivial networks

Imagination does not imply fallible fantasy, but rather it refers to perception, the perceived and the interweaving of narratives. It is a negotiation of being-becoming between memory, temporary manifestations, aspirations and the possible. Imagination can project being-becoming into a perceived historical 'reality' and into a perceived present 'reality', but more critically imagination can project being-becoming into a multiplicity of futures and possible futures (Bhiel and Lock 2017). Thereafter imagination can bring the various projected being-becoming into conversation with each other. Imagination and the related ideoscapes hold incredible power, because they inform sense making, meaning making and being-becoming. In addition, the imagination and ideoscapes are key contributors to the construction of communities, social connectivity and temporary manifestations (Appadurai 1996). However, ideoscapes and imagination are not entirely emancipatory or formless forces in their functioning or their role in being-becoming (Appadurai 1996). The imagination is informed by communities or those who have the resources to perpetuate particular imagination works. Imagination and the mobility of imagination is impacted by the ability or the space to practise these mental workings and transferals. Imagination lives in the mind and is embodied in the physical. Thus, power dynamics in 'realities' have an effect on imagination and the politics of imagination.

The Tunisian youth utilised electronic mediums to publicise the confrontations with the police in order to expose the political repression and the brutality of the Ben Ali regime. Almost instantaneously, tweets, Facebook messages and YouTube videos with images of young protestors being violently attacked by police reached millions of electronic medium users and its ideoscape viewers across Tunisia and abroad. The state could no longer confine events, repress communication and regulate being-becoming. The mobility of these imaginative works triggered tremendous outrage and stimulated the Tunisian populace to join the uprising. The uprising, particularly street protests, mushroomed all over the country, which reflects the dispersed imagined communities that electronic mediums facilitate. The decentralisation of the uprising reflects the individual engagement with imaginative works and their role in fuelling agency.

Aside from electronic mediums' ability to outmanoeuvre state repression, there were underlying reasons that drew the Tunisian population into this mediascape. The usage of the word media in mediascapes can be misleading. The mind jumps to news outlets and social media platforms like Facebook or Twitter. However, 'media' in this particular usage with mediascapes refers to the medium of communication and the type of transferal (Appadurai 1996). Bearing in mind that the focus is on the medium, it should be noted that there are platforms or organisations that produce, facilitate and advocate the particular medium and can also have a hand in creating the content, the ideoscape, which is circulated through the medium. The varying types of mediums within a mediascape take on various formations and are created with particular types of functions or means of functioning, which are historically and contextually situated. Mediums can gain relevance or lose relevance within a populace as well as never gaining relevance. It then leads one to beg the question of why a *particular* medium in the mediascape become a pinnacle tool in the Tunisian revolution. There is a plurality of mediums in the mediascape, but electronic mediums, such as the internet with its various platforms, and technological means of communicating arose as the prominent mediums in Tunisia. In addition to their prominence, they were utilised as mechanisms for furthering the revolution. Why did the Tunisian populace turn to electronic mediums and technological forms of communication? What influenced this turn and the resulting prominence? Electronic mediums and online social networks stand out against other mediascapes and forms of connecting, communicating and moving ideoscapes. While electronic mediums appear similar to other mediascapes in that technology acts as the vehicle for imagination and connection, electronic mediums are marked by their accelerated and malleable movement (Appadurai 1996). Thus, information about the events of the revolution travelled faster than the state could exert control over, and the intimacy of receiving unedited footage of police brutality unleashed a wave of angered sentiment that contributed to the mobilisation of the youth.

Electronic mediums can close or lessen the experiential distance between the agent and an imaginative work, but more particularly electronic mediums can close or lessen the experiential distance between a viewer and an imaginative work presenting an event or temporary manifestation (Appadurai 1996). Electronic mediums hold the resources to make, to circulate and to experience an imaginative work's subjectivity as if it were the viewer's, or the consumer's, own personal experiences. Closing the experiential distance makes it possible for the viewer to resonate with the imaginative work, which contributes to the sharing and negotiations with the various imaginations and ideoscapes circulated through electronic mediums. It can allow for connectivity between agents or communities that previously were not imagined or imagined possible. However, the particular assemblage of electronic mediums and online social networks did not inherently have the power or ability to incite a revolution. The assemblage synergised materials to extend what people were already doing or wanted to do. The assemblage is designed to be a tool wherein ideoscapes can travel. A moment of critical reflection is needed to reveal the underlying trap with extending human capabilities. Technology is made and epistemologically framed to appear objective and ahistorical, but it is deeply situated in subjectivity as technology is built for a specific audience or a certain construct of society (Mavhunga 2017). Technology does not simply get transferred into another locality or imagined community. The designed functions and assemblage of the technology can be reimagined, negotiated, repurposed and attributed possibility for it to cater as a more applicable tool in the respective context (Mavhunga 2017).

In the Tunisian context, there is evidence of technological mediums facilitating the reimagining of community forming. An alliance developed between urban middle-class youth and the unemployed youth from the interior regions of Tunisia that experienced the flipside of the state's implementation and development of being. The protesting youths spoke across the regional – which can also be translated into economic – divide created by the state's policies. After forming a convivial network, the protesting youth utilised the differing components of being-becoming to aid in mobilising the shared aspiration for being-becoming. It can be seen in groups of youth cyber activists, from the developed coastal region of Tunis, physically moving into their convivial network into the interior regions to contribute their set of skills to the mobilisation. The efficiency of the convivial network in combination with electronic mediums helped transform a series of demonstrations in Sidi Bouzid into a national uprising and from thereon spilling over onto the international networks. With spilling over onto international networks, it notes the mobility of imagination that electronic mediums enable. This mobility of imagination across nation-state boundaries caused a series of nation states, like Egypt or Libya, to renegotiate their regulated and structural being-becoming with the youth's being-becoming or the aspirations thereof. While the international spread of youth protests did not necessarily result in change of regime or state being-becoming, it was signalling the youths' commitment to their assemblages of being-becoming and the power the youth has at their disposal to follow through on that commitment (Honwana 2013).

Online social networks facilitated the sharing of imaginations between the Tunisian populace, which virtually created an imagined community and imagined conviviality that manifested as a heterogeneous group of activists who took the protests to the street. This heterogeneous group had no clear leadership and mobilised as a convivial network (Honwana 2013). The convivial network between the Tunisian protesters that was made through virtual connectivity, relationships and interdependences allowed a previously repressed populace to negotiate the various formations of being-becoming, which were monopolised by the nation state. Being-becoming with the accompanying incompleteness is the currency of conviviality (Nyamnjoh 2017). Conviviality, which can be superficially understood as interdependence, encourages the building of social networks, where the agents can explore ways of enhancing or complementing themselves and each other via the varying manifestations of being-becoming and the possible or the imagined (Nyamnjoh 2017).

Self-making and multiplicity

The Tunisian uprising hit the electronic mediums and online social networks in 'real time', or seemingly instantaneously. The Tunisian youth utilised the acceleration and malleability of electronic mediums to publicise the populace's outrage and mobilising convivial networks. However, there is a point of sharing and engagement of ideoscapes within the electronic mediums. The sharing of repressed narratives, aspirations for being-becoming, and imagined being-becoming was facilitated by the particular assemblage of electronic mediums and online social networks. The linked virtual being-becoming on this mediascape also brought forth new potential and possibility for being-becoming and the assembling of imagined communities.

Electronic mediums and online social networks, while offering unique resources and means to navigate temporary manifestation, also constructed a cyberspace, virtual connectivity and resources to experiment with self-making and being-becoming (Appadurai 1996). The experimentation with self-making and being-becoming was not limited to the plausible, the predictable, the tangible or realism. The pinnacle component to this assemblage of electronic mediums and cyberspace is structurally centralising the project of self-imagining and being-becoming into the core operations (Appadurai 1996). The implied freedom of expression, imagination, communication and being-becoming offered tantalising potential to the Tunisian populace with this mediascapes development. Considering the pinnacle component and the mediascape's assemblage, it is unsurprising that this mediascape was used to share imagined being-becoming and later appropriated to unite a convivial network for an uprising against the state's dictations of being-becoming. Thus, cyberspace gradually facilitated the emergence of political contestation in both virtual spaces and the streets (Honwana 2013). Governmental abuses or atrocities and the outraged responses from the Tunisian people were circulated within the virtual social networks and through electronic mediums. This circulation exposed the nation state and distributed information about the Tunisian situation across spatiotemporal boundaries and past the state's repressive measures (Honwana 2013).

The ability for spatiotemporal transcendence of electronic media allowed for irregular and fluid imagined communities to be constructed. Electronic mediums and technological means of communicating are a central product of a specific construct of modernity, but they have become a defining factor of globalisation and the globalised world. It holds the ability to accentuate, facilitate and accelerate global flows and global networks within globalisation. Alongside this ability, the assemblage of electronic mediums and technological means of communicating are changing the constructs of space and the landscapes used as building blocks for imagined beings, imagined communities and imagined worlds (Appadurai 1996). Modifying the means of engagement, communication and interaction creates a ripple effect on formations of being-becoming and the possible negotiations of being-becoming. It alters the basis for being-becoming with the irregular formation of imagined communities across spatiotemporal restrictions and the presentation of a plurality of ideoscapes (Appadurai 1996). Electronic mediums presented a higher rate and a more subjective interaction with a multiplicity of being-becoming. The mediums presented scripts for being-becoming in that the communities across the world were also imagined, which generated and facilitated a larger selection of possible being-becoming (Appadurai 1996). Alongside the multiplicity of scripts, the sharing of imagination and the resulting imagined communities were constructed across spatiotemporal boundaries. This potential for scattered assemblages reflects in the orchestration and mobilisation of the Tunisian revolution. The uprising did not occur in one location, but rather scattered across the Tunisian nation state. The uprising was not a spearheaded attack, but rather a horizontal collective mobilisation that replicated the connective networks of electronic mediums. Similar to how the state could not shut down the content or the platforms appearing on electronic mediums, protest and protesters would merely surface in a new location (Honwana 2013). It was metaphorically like cutting off one head for two more to sprout.

Being-becoming is not marked by singularity or by completeness. Performances of being-becoming in temporary manifestations do not incorporate the entirety of being-becoming and potential being-becoming. It is possible for beings to not directly correspond or appear similarly across imagination, the intangible, and temporary manifestation. In the context of Tunisia, the state's vision for being and the support of the state's being was the only being-becoming that was allowed to exist. Applying the shadowlands and the theory of incompleteness, the state's vision of being could be gained, performed, reproduced by those that upheld the state and their system, who were practising and embodying structural forming agency. This vision of being did not allow for other imagined being-becoming to take on formation in temporary manifestations. It created a dissonance between imagined being-becoming and practised being-becoming, which highlights the importance of analysing beyond temporary manifestation and incorporating incompleteness. Building on Crenshaw (1991) critique of a singular narrative of identity, being-becoming does not appear in a singularity. Manifestations of being-becoming are interlocked with multifaceted, intangible, imagined and aspired being-becoming and the experiences of power dynamics. If being-becoming is understood as an overlapping, creolising, interacting multitude, the complex business of being-becoming allows for being-becoming to co-exist, conflict, interact, influence, appropriate and cause friction. Temporary manifestations of 'reality', and within the agents' themselves, are layered and nuanced being-becoming. Thus, being is and can be simultaneous beings. Beings can partially emerge or emerge intertwined. If there are multiple beings manifesting, there need to be degrees of becoming and multiple negotiations of becoming that can communicate with each other. Becoming does not necessarily incorporate the entirety of an actor's being or beings. Rather, these beings can undergo becoming separately, which allows for an actor to be simultaneously being and becoming.

The appearance of stifled imagined being-becoming and the multiplicity of being-becoming is marked by the unity found between the youth and the structural forming agents. Social forms partake and are shaped by multiple systems and forces in which they are themselves contingent and shifting (Biehl and Lock 2017). Biehl and Lock (2017: 10) stated that 'becoming demands more than flat realism of contextualization, determinism and historicism'.

Marginalisation and quasi-events

The Tunisian revolution was initiated by the Tunisian youth, but the mobilisation of the revolt was not spearheaded by a singular group (Honwana 2013). Rather, a collective sharing of imagination fuelled a broad call for action and protest across the seemingly separated imagined communities of Tunisia. As momentum built, other sectors of society joined in with the dissent. Labour unions and lawyers were the first to join the youth by staging their own protests in solidarity after the martyrdom (Honwana 2013). The Tunisian youth could be seen as liminal beings in previous theorisation of being-becoming by liminality. By definition, the youth exist within liminal space where they achieve specific social, political, biological and financial markers to transition into adulthood. Often these markers are indexical of the context wherein youth exist (Durham 2000). The youth are marginalised and seen to exist outside societal structures by liminality. However, being-becoming was not restricted to those at the outskirts of society. Being-becoming was undergone by those who constructed the imagined community of Tunisia. The constituents of the imagined community do not have to be equal, but each constituent plays a role in the assembling of the imagined community and the perceived structures; essentially the marginalised do not operate in chaos as they are a variable for shaping an assemblage.

The theory of assemblage concentrates on fluid formations of diversifying components and their social complexities, which allow for a multiplicity of beings and a more complex ability or more complex operations of being-becoming (Deleuze and Guattari 1987). However, these assemblages are not removed from being-becoming, but they are rather the resulting assembling-assemblages of being-becoming in temporary manifestations. The appearances of being-becoming, which in themselves are assemblages, in temporary manifestations can create and have created particular structural or systematic assemblages of being-becoming, such as globalisation and the nation state. These structural or systematic assemblages of being-becoming are embodied, practised, regulated and disciplined into existence (Foucault 1998). It must be noted that these assemblages are not abstracted into notions of structures, but rather deeply located in what can be understood as agency and the power dynamics surrounding agency (Anderson 1983). This means that a series of complex interactions between being-becoming, strategic agency and power dynamics were responsible for manifesting these assemblages in temporary manifestations. In addition, these assemblages and their formations rely on these complex interactions for existence, functionality, exchange and reassembling (Deleuze and Guattari 1987). These strategically preformed assemblages of being-becoming can promote, enforce and influence being-becoming. Despite the seemingly contradicting interconnections, the communication across being-becoming and the resulting assemblages are possible with being-becoming held as a multiplicity, which grapples with the variables of being-becoming beyond contextualisation, determinism and historicism. Being-becoming then gains the ability to partake in structural being-becoming while including the ability to imagine new 'realities' or possible forms of being-becoming that are not necessarily a reaction to structural being-becoming and structural assemblages.

Two particular systematic or structural assemblages appear prominently in the context of the Tunisian revolution. Both assemblages, globalisation and the nation state, reflect the undertaking and performance of being-becoming by the uprising populace. Engaging with these two assemblages and their formations, it is possible to gain insight into the being-becoming that these assemblages facilitate and how those assemblages have been negotiated or appropriated by Tunisian agents to achieve their aspired being-becoming. It is important to reiterate that the notion of assemblages and the shadowlands do not aim to argue that there are no formations of boundaries or divides, but rather it aims to argue that a particular assemblage dictates whether there is a boundary and what is the nature of that boundary. With the assemblage of globalisation, globalisation gains its configuration by the relationship between five dimensions of global flows: ethnoscapes, mediascapes, technoscapes, financescapes and ideoscapes. The relationships between these flows manifest complex translocal and transnational processes, where being forms malleable nodes in the fluid matrix (Appadurai 1996). Imagination is centralised in the assemblage of globalisation, or global flows, through its vital role in agency. Agency travels through, shapes and negotiates the relationship between the five dimensional flows (Appadurai 1996). Thereby it affects the forms of being-becoming within the matrix of connectivity. Despite the fluidity of globalisation, it does create boundaries, but these assemblages take on a porous, irregular and malleable nature. There is a marked mobility of the assemblage and the linked boundaries, but this mobility is not emancipated or equal as the power dynamics within the assemblage of globalisation advocate and allow greater ability for a particular imagined being to move through its boundaries or enter into negotiations of being-becoming (Appadurai 1996). In addition, this assemblage of globalisation is marked by a defining factor of electronic mediums and technological means of communication, which was purposefully constructed to allow for engagement and experimentation of being-becoming (Appadurai 1996). In contrast to the assemblage of globalisation, the assemblage of the nation state strongly constructs boundaries that are highly regulated, controlled and maintained. The nation state gains its legitimisation and creates its imagined community by a strongly constructed boundary that is demarcated geographically (Anderson 1983). In addition, this creation and legitimisation uses physical structures and strategic agency to perpetuate this disjunctive space and formation of community. The concept of the nation state has been idealised as a cohesive and equal community with deep and horizontal comradeship, but the idealisation of the nation state brushes over how inequality and exploitation feature into the nation-state assemblage (Anderson 1983). The idealised assemblage of the nation state fails to capture the variety and complexity of being-becoming that exist in the imagined community of the nation state. As a result, it positions being, that does not correlate with the ideal being, at the margins of a society or to be society's marginalised. It draws boundaries or division between beings and creates a structure–chaos dichotomy, which allows for the erasure and the disappearance of experiences around being-becoming in theoretical works. The formation of boundaries and divides from an assemblage is performed and manifested through strategic agency, but these assemblages, nor the related boundaries, are not complete, fixed or necessarily separate from other assemblages (Deleuze and Guattari 1987).

Deleuze and Guattari (1987) metaphorically framed the theory of assemblage using the imagery of stars in the night sky and constellations. An assemblage is similar to a constellation due to the selective grouping of articulations in a particular and identifiable pattern. However, this constellation, and thus assemblages, does not lose its relationship with the bodies around it. On the other hand, the formation of an assemblage shapes the means of which connection, communication, negotiation and interaction can occur with exterior assemblages (Deleuze and Guattari 1987). There is an assembly of assemblages that is in a fluctuating, multifaceted state of being-becoming, where there are varying degrees of being-becoming, formations of being-becoming, imaginations of being-becoming and negotiations of being-becoming across the various assemblages. The various assemblages can influence, appropriate, merge, clash or engage with other assemblages, especially as assemblages overlap and layer temporary manifestations. In the context of the Tunisian revolution, two assemblages, globalisation and the nation state, come into friction with one another via the practised agency and being-becoming of the Tunisian protesters. The assemblages came into friction with one another due to the Tunisian population drawing on the potentiality and functionality of the globalisation assemblage to change the nation state's monopoly on being-becoming. The Tunisian population lives within a matrix of assemblages, where they are all constituents in the construction of an assemblage. Notions of erasure or marginalisation inform the assembling of these assemblages. In conjunction, these constituents are concurrently informing and assembling a multiplicity of differing structures.

Aside from sidestepping the restrictiveness of structure–agency and structure–chaos dichotomies, the renegotiation of these preceding epistemological frameworks around being-becoming is vital to demonstrate and encompass being-becoming in the everyday, everywhere and quasi-events. Being-becoming is not confined to special or marginalised expressive spaces. Instead, the project of being-becoming can feature into the ordinary, subconscious and insignificant mental work of the 'everyday' person (Appadurai 1996). Electronic mediums in the context of Tunisia perpetuate and reveal the implementation of being-becoming in the 'everyday' person. The medium appeared in the majority of homes or via personal technology, where the access to this medium publicised in data the formation and sharing of being-becoming in the everyday (Honwana 2013). Later, it was this 'everyday' usage of electronic mediums that dropped the straw to break the camel's back. Mohamed Bouazizi was not the first Tunisian youth to commit self-immolation, but it was the collective of 'everyday' negotiations of being-becoming that finally sparked the mobilisation against the nation state (Honwana 2013). The prior conceptualisation of structures overlooks the significance of quasi-events and embodiment of institutional being, or 'structures', responsible for the construction of 'reality', and the social change or negotiation occurring within institutional or societal organisation previously seen as 'structures'. Structures are not fixed or only open to change by outside agents, or outsiders. The epistemological shift attributes more dimensions and nuances to agency and being-becoming for the Tunisian population.

Conclusion

Electronic mediums, in conjunction with the analytical framework of the shadowlands, reveal a more complex nature around being-becoming and to some degree it facilitates the complexity of being-becoming. It, firstly, centres the notion of self-making at its core functioning, but then provides a greater multiplicity of being through offering, increasing accessibility, and publicising the various manifestations of being-becoming. It then provides the resources for a particularly intimate and immersive means to share and engage with the ideoscapes and imaginations of being-becoming. Secondly, electronic mediums have the ability to transcend spatiotemporal boundaries, and in this context of Tunisia, state repression or monopolies on being-becoming. The spatiotemporal transcendence facilitates a scattered and fluid connectivity that results in the irregular formation of imagined communities. These imagined communities can then be mobilised as convivial networks as the Tunisian uprising reveals. In addition, electronic mediums highlight the 'everyday' practice and the quasi-events linked into assemblages and manifestations of being-becoming. The practice of being-becoming is not static or limited to moments of forceful transformation.

References

Anderson, B. (2006 [1983]) *Imagined communities: Reflections on the origin and spread of nationalism*, London and New York: Verso.

Appadurai, A. (1996) 'Here and now', in A. Appadurai, *Modernity at large: Cultural dimensions of globalization*, Minneapolis and London: University of Minnesota Press, pp. 1–23.

Biehl, J. and Lock, P. (2017) *The Anthropology of Becoming*, Durham: Duke University Press.

Crenshaw, K. (1991) 'Mapping the Margins: Intersectionality, Identity Politics, and Violence against Women of Color', *Stanford Law Review*, Vol. 43, No. 6, pp. 1241–99.

Deleuze, G. and Guattari, F. (1987) *A thousand plateaus* (Trans. by Brain Massumi), Minneapolis: The University of Minnesota Press.

Durham, D. (2000) 'Youth and the Social Imagination in Africa, Part 1', *Anthropological Quarterly*, Vol. 73, No. 3, pp. 113-120.

Mavhunga, C. C. (ed.) (2017) *What do science, technology and innovation mean from Africa?* Cambridge: Massachusetts Institute of Technology Press.

Nyamnjoh, F. B. (2017) 'Incompleteness: Frontier Africa and the currency of conviviality', *Journal of Asian and African Studies*, Vol. 52, No. 3, pp. 253–70.

Chapter 5

The Democratic Republic of Congo (DRC): A Multi-layered Shadowlands

Remi Calleja

Introduction

Contextualisation

The introduction written by our group attempts to explain the emergence of the concept of shadowlands. Thus, after the analysis of the applicability, limitations and conceptualisations of the concepts of liminality, borderlands and crossroads, a need for a new analytical tool was felt among our panel of students. With the intention to move beyond binary oppositions and dichotomies, characteristic of the Western framework of knowledge, we have proposed the shadowlands as a concept to expand on and incorporate the various conceptualizations of being, becoming, and being-becoming. Two main axes lead the epistemological framework of the concept: the idea of incompleteness, which implies a constant negotiation and renegotiation of boundaries, a capacity to continually renew itself; and the three-dimensional narrative, which contrasts with the idea of unilinearity implied by the metaphors of the precedent concepts and limiting their possibilities.

Situations of shadowlands, also drawing from the possibilities of liminality, crossroads and borderlands, are experienced in many ways, existing at different levels. They can be conceived in geographical terms, attached to the physical realm, as well as in social terms, with a more figurative/symbolic approach.

Methodology and objectives

In this chapter, I seek to display the different applications of the shadowlands in a nation that has faced and is still facing a situation of transition. Thus, in the specific postcolonial society that the DRC represents, I aim to depict the articulation of these spaces of junctions, as well as the various ways undertaken by Congolese people and communities to navigate within. Indeed, the 'maelstrom of aggravating political and economic crises' (De Boeck and Plissart 2004: 75) that characterises the Democratic Republic of the Congo appears to link the nation and its political and economic contexts directly with the concept of shadowlands outlined in the introduction. Moreover, religious and social aspects must also be analysed. Today, societies are understood as holistic and dynamic spaces in which spheres are mingling, interwoven and constantly interacting. It is not possible to isolate a particular field.

Built on the analysis of five ethnographies, this chapter mobilises different dichotomies (traditional/modern, continuity/change, forest/village, life/death, rural/urban, local/global …). The overtaking of these various binary oppositions is pivotal in the argument around shadowlands. In the Congolese situation, a constant negotiation between opposite poles is at stake, indeed, blurring the idea of opposition. Thus, I intend to understand how these different notions are reconciled within a given society; how social agents navigate between their tradition and the colonial input, between the rural and the urban, between life and death …; and finally, how cultural politics are simultaneously an enterprise of legitimisation, as well as a challenging project to the dominant discourse.

In order to build and structure my argument, I will study the five following ethnographies:

Kinshasa: Tales of the Invisible City, written by Filip De Boeck in 2004, presents an account of the numerous situations of crisis interwoven experienced by Kinois. The author, through an analysis that goes beyond the mere focus on the African metropolis, provides simultaneously, physical and tangible narratives around the urban reality experienced, as well as stories from the invisible city, projections of imaginaries and beliefs of the inhabitants. The physical and invisible worlds emerge as tightly interwoven, constantly interacting with each other. The piece underlines the blurriness of frontiers and the erosion of dichotomies through the different situations, spaces and people presented.

Rene Devisch collaborated with Claude Brodeur to write *The Law of the Lifegivers: The Domestication of Desire* in 1999. This exchange between an anthropologist and a psychoanalyst focuses on Yaka people, emphasising the importance of the body and space in their cosmology. Different life-giving and life-threatening figures are presented, especially the sorcerer, the diviner, the therapist and the chief. They emerge as shadowlands figures, or Tricksters, navigating between worlds and across boundaries. More than a crossroads figure,[3] the Trickster embodies the nature of the shadowlands itself, which is a space where order and norms are disrupted and new order

[3] See Chapter 1, pp. 20-21.

and norms are then created and adopted. 'Neither good, nor bad, nor neutral the Trickster breaks down order by introducing chaos, but simultaneously, also brings harmony and order to chaos'. As the shadowlands, the mysterious character overreaches the mere dichotomy between two worlds, and therefore, represents an infinity of possibilities. 'The mythical personage is simultaneously, in all the worlds of possibility, and between them eluding categorisation. The Trickster, never fully in one place, is a being that opens up the possibility for many realities to intersect'.[4] It is not only a being of the shadowlands but also embodies the shadowlands itself. Finally, the dialogue established between the two scholars, although sometimes conflictual, eventually permits to overcome dichotomies, re-think frontiers and boundaries, and distance ourselves from the hegemony of the Western dominant framework of knowledge. Indeed, through the analysis of situations and figures linked with our concept of shadowlands, alternative forms of knowledge emerge. Thus, shadowlands are representative of the situations analysed as well as of the paper produced in itself.

In 1996, Johannes Fabian and Tshibumba Kanda Matulu worked together to publish *Remembering the Present: Painting and Popular History in Zaire*. Through paintings, a historical narrative is created, underlining the various ambiguous situations of the country. The context permits to grasp the idea of shadowlands in both the past and present DRC. Indeed, the history of the 'Zaire' is 'painted' as complex, chaotic and constantly reshaping itself. The non-linear narrative created by the artist and historian

---

[4] Ibid.

Tshibumba, a man who also joggles with frontiers and goes beyond strict categorisations and conceptions of the history, underlines the entanglement of past, present and future. Each layer of time directly impacts the others.

Pouvoir Traditionnel et Pouvoir d'Etat en Republique Democratique du Congo is Héritier Mambi Tunga-Bau's thesis written in 2010. With an emphasis on politics, the argument focuses on the negotiation of the different powers in the DRC. Traditional and national authorities co-exist, simultaneously opposing and nourishing each other.

Finally, Bob White proposes in *Rumba Rules: The Politics of Dance Music in Mobutu's Zaire* (2008) an exciting approach of the relationship between politics and popular music in the DRC. Cultural politics is presented as both an enterprise of legitimisation and resistance to the ruling national power. This formidable ethnography states the importance of music in the shaping of societies, overcoming categorisations and dichotomies and establishing bonds between frontiers. The role of music, and arts in general, cannot be neglected in social sciences. These mediums are clearly embedded in other fields such as politics, economy and the organisation of the social life in general. Music and musicians invest characteristics of the shadowland, embodying the figure of the Trickster.

Thus, drawing from each book, cross-cutting themes emerge, as well as specific approaches to the various situations. Different analyses and interpretations can be established, always in relationships with the concept of shadowlands. The ethnographies permit simultaneously to reinforce universals in the conception of the new analytical tool, within the context of the DRC, and to unveil specific approaches. Indeed, different applications of the shadowlands are presented through this chapter, all constitutive of the situation of crisis and chaos experienced by the nation. Nevertheless, I am not proposing to give an exhaustive list of the possible applications of shadowlands, the enterprise would be unrealisable, especially because of the multi-layered nature of the concept and its faculty to constantly renew itself. I rather focus on particular cases in which this analytical tool emerges as central and particularly relevant. Thus, the different themes directly related to the shadowlands that I present permit a deeper insight of the general concept, clarifying the overarching point made in our common introduction.

Through the chapter, the fluid character of the concept is obvious. Indeed, every concept mingles, the different features can be found in different parts, always unveiling new aspects. Thus, there are no clear-cut boundaries and separation between the ideas raised, which make the arguments of the work a form of 'epistemological shadowlands'.

Overall, this chapter intends to unveil different sources of knowledge, challenging the Western dominant discourse that has regularly structured intellectual works so far. It also aims to underline the conception of shadowlands through different narratives, through various points of view (the colonial lens, scholars' perspective and from the various Congolese communities). In that respect, the five ethnographies, written by different authors, have been chosen to cover various fields and different intellectual frameworks. Furthermore, more than only embedded within the specific situations analysed and depicted, shadowlands are integrative parts of the various works produced, as well as integrative parts of this very particular chapter. The pieces, including mine, produce 'epistemological shadowlands', negotiating and overcoming borders and categories.

Questions and thesis

From the readings, a set of problematics emerge. These questions build the directive lines of the chapter. First, how does the concept of shadowlands emerge through the different narratives studied? How is it relevant in the specific context? What are the characteristics or approaches of the concept brought to the fore?

Other inquiries can concern the different dichotomies perceived: how are the modern and the traditional articulated in the DRC? How is the idea of cultural politics simultaneously built to legitimise and challenge the national power?

Overall, what are the tensions and the negotiations that rise in the situation analysed? Finally, what are the responses and the potentialities liberated by these points of junctions to overcome the chaotic situation specific to the nation?

Roadmap

This chapter is organised into three core parts. First, an insight into the history of the DRC permits to contextualise and, thus, to grasp the different logics that cross the space studied.

Then, the analysis continues based on two main axes. The first axis focuses on the physical, material nature emerging from situations linked to ambiguous spaces. At first, shadowlands appear as inscribed in the physical realm. They are spaces, cities, places … Ideas of movement and mobility are central to the understanding of the concept.

The place of the body also emerges as pivotal, introducing a possible mingling between worlds.

The argument of the second axis is built to emphasise the intertwining of the various social spheres. 'Shadowlands' is a concept in which categories are mingling, such as the political, the social, the economic and the religious. It overcomes the limits of the physical order, permeating every layer and world. The articulation of being and becoming is analysed through politics, the everyday life, as well as ritual practices.

Finally, the last part focuses on the emerging figures and possible responses that arise from these situations of chaos. The creativity, openness and possible adaptations that shadowlands imply are at the heart of the conclusion. I introduce the various reactions to re-establish an order, or also to blossom within disorder. It permits to open the research to the projection of possible evolutions of this context of multiple interwoven shadowlands. My personal take-away completes the conclusion.

DRC: a complex history

The Chinese philosopher Confucius said 'study the past if you would define the future'. History is an ambiguous field. Indeed, the discipline represents the study of the past, justifying a present and projecting toward a possible future. History is dynamic and governed by interactions. At the crossroads, history is also the repository of different logics simultaneously challenging each other and interacting together: the art of storytelling and the written mode. This short historical background of the Congo reflects the idea – the two logics both completing and challenging each other. Built on Tshibumba Kanda Matulu's paintings and comments (Fabian 1996), the part mobilised the art of storytelling. At a junction point, storytellers 'do not only tell the history, they are themselves a settled history'[5] (Bazin 1979: 436). Moreover, the artist overcomes the limits of being exclusively a painter or a storyteller, stating 'I am an artist, yes. I am a historian'[6] (Fabian 1996: 9). Through his analysis of Kinshasa, De Boeck permits to justify the choice of presenting a painted, nonlinear history in the context of the DRC. Indeed:

> in the absence of a canonized history, collective social memory was and is at liberty to annex more of the cultural space to develop its own, nonlinear, heterogeneous dynamics in which there is room for difference and openness. This is, for example, the space occupied by the popular genres of music, theatre and painting. (De Boeck and Plissart 2004: 91)

Additions from various scholars who embody the second logic also complete Tshibumba's version of the popular history of Zaire.

In *Remembering the Present*, a book structured as a dialogue between Johannes Fabian and Tshibumba, the three first paintings depict the Zaire of the ancestors, the prehistory of Congo. The importance of the landscape is stressed, as 'the first thing in a history of Zaire' (ibid: 18).

---

[5] In French in the text: 'ne disent plus seulement l'histoire, ils sont eux-mêmes une histoire sédimentée'.

[6] In this case, the term 'historian' should be understood from a Western perspective: a person who studies and writes the past through the Western school of thought.

The passage from prehistory to history represents a process of imagination and re-composition from the artist-historian. Banza Kongo, the supposed ruler of the Kingdom of Kongo,[7] is presented as the first to interact with the Portuguese newcomers. He also symbolises, through his death, the taking over of the region from King Leopold II, the founder of the Congo Free State. In reality, the figure of Banza Kongo is 'the embodiment of African civilization' (ibid: 271), representing a period that spreads from the end of the fifteenth to the nineteenth century. Fabian's comments add precision to Tshibumba narratives. Indeed, it is Nzinga Kwulu who hosted the Portuguese navigator Diogo Cao in 1487. The Congolese ruler eventually sent an embassy to Portugal, which brought back missionaries, soldiers, craftsmen and presents.

That early history of the Congo reflects the several interactions with foreigners (Portuguese, Arabs, Belgians …), as well as the numerous kingdoms that populated the region (Kete, Luba, Lunda …). The particular space was shared, representing a zone of contacts, and could be considered as shadowlands, a junction area between different logics colliding. Ethnic conflicts, confusion of power, as well as interactions, contacts and creativity, shaped the early history painted by Tshibumba. No power appeared authoritative and dominant enough to establish laws and introduce 'order'.

Then, King Leopold II of Belgium declared the Congo Free State in 1885, implementing the colonial rule. The painter explains that 'once they had replaced Banza Kongo there was no way out; we lived in slavery. Our sovereignty

[7] Dominant force until the Portuguese arrival, it existed from the 14th to the early 19th centuries.

died right there' (ibid: 36). However, in his thesis, Héritier Mambi Tunga-Bau nuances this perspective, explaining that from the Leopoldian colonialism until today, the state authority has never completely denied traditional powers (Mambi Tunga-Bau 2010: 42).

Following the exclusive control of Leopold II, the Congo became a Belgian colony in 1908. The Leopoldian colonialism followed by the colonial era presented different crises such as various conflicts (between the *Force Publique* and Italians, the Tetela revolt ...), assassinations of Congolese leaders (Chief Lumpungu, Colonel Kokolo ...), and popular uprising (Miner's strikes, Patrice Lumumba leading the uprising in January 1959). This era also saw the arrival of 'modernity',[8] as concrete industrial innovations with the building of railroads, the establishment of the Mining Company, the various monuments erected, and on a more symbolic level, with the trial and imprisonment of the religious leader, Simon Kimbangu, considered a threat to the established order and to the European modernity.

This period of harsh domination ended with Patrice Lumumba signing the Act of Independence on 30 June 1960. The independence was set during the 'Table ronde de Bruxelles' earlier that year, gathering Congolese political figures and traditional authorities with Belgian political and economic leaders (Fabian 1996; Mambi Tunga-Bau 2010). Nevertheless, through Tshibumba's painting of the postcolonial era, the transition appears just as conflictual as the time preceding. Indeed, various regions declared

---

8 Modernity here is understood according to the postmodernism school of thought, especially through processes of industrialisation, urbanisation, secularisation, rejection of 'traditions' and importation of a particular economic system: the capitalism.

themselves independent (Katanga and South Kasai), ethnic conflicts carried on and assassinations of potential threats continued. Thus, Lumumba, freshly dismissed from his Prime Minister role, was killed on 17 January 1961. It is during the mandate of Joseph Kasa-Vubu at the head of the nation (1960–1965) that the Lieutenant General Mobutu, commander in chief of the army, took control and declared himself president. The mid-1970s saw changes in international markets that influenced the local economy of the country. During the following decade, a strong democratic denial took place in relation to multipartyism (White 2008). These conflictual times appear as shadowlands, with confusion, contradictions, oppositions of power, ambiguous systems of rules and laws, but also creativity and emergences of new figures and opportunists. The ambivalence of the concept proposed emerges from this history of Congo/Zaire.

The naming of the country, by the way, has changed through eras. 'Zaire existed since the days of old' (Fabian 1996: 17). Tshibumba believes 'it was 'Zaire' in those times' (ibid: 22). Renamed Congo through the influence of Leopold II (Congo Free State), apparently to pay tribute to Banza Kongo, the name remains until Mobutu's seizure of power. With the democratic transition following Mobutu's period as head of the state, the Democratic Republic of Congo was established.

The early 1990s appeared to be a response to Mobutu's total control, with the emergence of multipartyism (De Boeck and Plissart 2004). The riots of 1991, known as *le pillage*, are remembered by many Congolese as a 'low point in economic and political history and as a symbol of how deeply *le mal zairois* had penetrated society' (White 2008: 3).

When, in 1997, the 'Léopard du Zaïre'[9] was chased away, a hope for a democratic transition was raised. Mobutu's dismissal eventually ended the first civil war (1996–1997). The military empowered through alliances, Lauren Desire Kabila 'and his troops marched triumphantly into Kinshasa in May 1997 [...]. The capital was buzzing with excitement' (ibid: 1). Nevertheless, the political and social situation of the country did not improve, the transition appearing in a constant state of incompleteness, especially with the continuation of conflicts, wars and inter-ethnic confrontations. With the deterioration of the relations with his allies, Kabila could not avoid the outburst of the second civil war (1999–2003). In 2001, he 'was assassinated under mysterious circumstances and succeeded by his son Joseph, who early on made clear his intentions to revive the peace process' (ibid: xxii). The first multi-party election took place in 2003, however, 'armed conflict and violence had become endemic' to the region (ibid: xxii). The head of the nation has managed to exceed his mandate as he is still in power today.[10]

The country is still facing numerous conflicts, popular uprisings and tensions, reinforcing the incompleteness of the transitional process. Indeed, White presents 'a political transition that has become a permanent way of life' (ibid: 239).

---

[9] Leopard of Zaire, Eagle of Kawele and Papa Marechal were different nicknames attributed to Mobutu.

[10] However, Jospeh Kabila announced that he would not run for re-elections that were scheduled to be held at the end of 2018. Nevertheless, that does not necessarily imply a more democratic political regime to come.

Shadowlands in the material world

The various metaphors explored in our general introduction (liminal thresholds, crossroads, borderlands and shadowlands) are embedded in the spatial realm. Thus, the first argument drawn from the specific ethnographies analysed is the spatial and material character of the different situations of shadowlands represented. Three principal axes reinforce the theme: shadowlands as places, the constant mobility attached to shadowlands and the relation between shadowlands and the body.

Shadowlands as physical places

In the introduction of *Kinshasa. Tales of the Invisible City*, Filip De Boeck describes beach Ngobila as 'a cannibalistic space which swallows everyone' (De Boeck and Plissart 2004: 15). Also presented as an 'industrial wasteland' (ibid: 15), the beach is a place of contrast, oppositions and extremes, physical shadowlands. Expanding his lens to the entire city, the Belgian professor of anthropology continues his narrative by presenting Kinshasa as 'a constant border-crossing phenomenon, resisting fixture, refusing capture' (ibid: 19). Thus, overcoming the metaphor of linearity and direction, which has limited other concepts such as liminality, crossroads and borderlands, Kinshasa represents a space not possible to capture or enclose. Contrasting with Leopoldville, developed along axes and segregated lines, Kinshasa refuses the universal metrics that have enabled a practical set of tools for colonial rules.

Indeed, from the colonisers' perspective, precolonial spaces were shadowlands, lands to be seized where different outsider groups could fight in order to establish a system and to bring order and civilisation. Invaders defined arbitrary borders, mapping the colonies to civilise and rule the darkness and contingence. The input of the colonialist modernity was, at first, a process of domestication and control. On the other hand, through the indigenous lens, established colonies were seen as 'exploitative "space[s] of death"' (ibid: 27).

These interactions between the supposed darkness and contingence of precolonial states and the enlightenment and order of colonies led to the dichotomy between village and forest. Originally, the separation was embedded with the opposition between the rural and the urban. The village, space of culture and structured system represented the world of the living, the human realm, contrasted with the forest, world of ambiguity and darkness, in which death and supernatural entities were dwelling (Devisch and Brodeur 1999; De Boeck and Plissart 2004). The forest represented then the shadowlands.

Contemporary, in rites, village outskirts appear as privileged locations for divinatory séances, reasserting the supposed dichotomy between village and forest. However, ritual divinations establish discursive spaces, embedding the practice within a physical place of contacts, of mingling between worlds, entities (Devisch and Brodeur 1999). Nevertheless, the various situations encountered by the Congolese through their history, and the epistemological shift in social sciences has led to the blurring of boundaries and the overcoming of dichotomies. Indeed, urban and rural are interwoven, without clear boundaries. In Kinshasa, rural and urban logics are colliding. The formerly rural concept of hunting, bounded to the forest, becomes linked to the urban through the reshaping and renaming of places (especially bars redefined as villages). Moreover, the city is shared by the living and the dead. Day and night are mingling, with the human and supernatural worlds interwoven. Being is defined by its multiplicity. Cemeteries become pivotal, centres of exchanges and interactions between life and death. De Boeck (De Boeck and Plissart 2004) goes further, qualifying Kinshasa in its totality as a necropolis, a cemetery city. His documentary *Cemetery State* (2010) reflects the idea. A re-creation and re-appropriation of a space-time occur. The city is at a crossroads, it is a shadowland where dichotomies are collapsing, boundaries are blurred and systems are outreached. Kinshasa implies multiverse and multiplicity of being, so do shadowlands.

More than cemeteries, all the infrastructures of the city can be perceived as spaces of transition, movement, and contingence. Streets are re-appropriated, especially by the youth, and characterize a nomadic mode of existence. They are seen as spaces of freedom, in which rules are abrogated and redefined. Simultaneously embodiment of the modern and the traditional, streets are both spaces of alternative modernities and representation of the realm of the night, in which witchcraft blossoms. They are constantly re-shaped, defined by the idea of incompleteness. This unfinished and everlasting character is also found in the architecture and the numerous infrastructures that are in permanent states of construction. Fragments of houses are embedded in different rhythms and temporalities. De Boeck reasserts the idea of the cannibalistic city by describing the commune of Mount Ngafula, an unfinished city where people 'live in the skeletons of their frozen dreams of progress and grandeur' (De Boeck and Plissart 2004: 229).

Widening the lens to the other regions of the DRC, our analytical concept also permits to analyse spaces at the border. The case of the diamond trade is particularly interesting, the frontier between Congo and Angola being an embodiment of shadowlands. Within this in-between space, rules are revoked and re-appropriated. There, soldiers act according to their specific desire. Thus, to be protected from military retributions ephemeral families are built on the run. People are negotiating between the two nations, seeking for economic opportunities. Borders are spaces in-between, at the margins of the specific rules and laws of the neighbouring countries, hence the depiction of the Kwango region, bordering Angola, as a zone 'at the margins of the national political scene' (Devisch and Brodeur 1999: 4). Moreover, they are spaces of transmigration, with people, goods, information that are moving and navigating. Mobility is characteristic of the border and embedded in the idea of shadowlands. This importance of the movement is the focus of the next point.

Shadowlands, a concept on the move

The general introduction presents two interpretations of incompleteness. In some sense, it is the removal of boundaries. While in others, it highlights the blurring, movement, intermingling and porous nature of these boundaries. Going further, the analytical tool implies a 'fluid and malleable nature'.[11] Possibilities for borrowing, trading and multiple beings emerge. Entities navigate to, within and out of this space of junctions. Moreover, shadowlands are themselves mobile entities, unfinished, in

---

[11] See Chapter 1, p. 42.

a constant state of motion and reconstruction. They have the capacity to renew themselves constantly. Through the ethnographies, mobility appears as a transversal both for the situations depicted and for the elements within, reinforcing the idea of shadowlands in the DRC.

Common to many former colonies, the problem of land is central in the Congo. People have been displaced, leading to a popular sense of insecurity, deterritorialisation and loss of place. A rupture has been implemented between the Congolese and their territory, inserting the population in a liminal space, neither here nor there. Thus, mobility has permeated both the reality and imagination of the inhabitants (De Boeck and Plissart 2004).

The mobile aspect of the DRC and of its components (people, communities, institutions …) is reflected in Tshibumba's history of Zaire. Indeed, many of the paintings represent travel axes and places linked to transport. Railways, planes, roads and cars are abundant through his narrative (Fabian 1996). It displays an idea of migration, transmigration and movement that seems profoundly rooted in the history of the country. To go further, the paintings present modernity as a factor of movement. Then, Western input in African culture could be seen as a point of entry to situations of shadowlands. The first pieces depicting the land of ancestors are calm and clearly set while the later history is a space-time of mingling, movements and confusion.

Artists, such as Tshibumba, embody the Trickster figure; a figure that is embedded in shadowlands. Franco, for example, the co-founder and leader of O.K. Jazz, was also well known for his 'marginal position in society' (White 2008: 136). In his analysis of music in the DRC, Bob White explains that 'any attempt to talk about the role of musicians in African society must address not only the social position of musicians but also their mobility relative to other social-occupational categories' (ibid: 131). Not only concerned with social mobility, musicians are also embedded in physical movement, travels and migrations. Indeed, becoming famous is a worldwide enterprise. The audience to entertain is always growing in number, leading to the expansion of tours' itineraries from local communities to the global world. Music is exported with the intention to reach other regions, countries and continents. Moreover, to expand their knowledge and approaches, musicians travel. Papa Wemba, the Congolese superstar, started to move regularly to Paris in the late 1970s. Through the years, his music became cross-influenced (with African, European and Cuban influences). Finally, 'foreign musicians have a long history in Zairian music' (ibid: 147). Importation of instruments, technologies and sounds are pivotal. Figures of shadowlands, musicians are embedded in mobility. Constantly shaping their music, themselves and the world in which they play, they need to travel, seeking for wider audiences and international fame. They impact the environment as much as the environment impacts them.

In the city, streets, as presented by De Boeck (De Boeck and Plissart 2004), reflect a nomadic existence. It is mainly the youth, 'relegated to sites of exclusion', who move into streets to dwell in an environment that can be seen as zones of movement par excellence, points of passage composed by crossroads, axes. The youth, not only limited to embody a site of exclusion, is also prominently present in urban public spaces, re-appropriating the surroundings. It implies ideas of incompleteness and ambivalence attached to shadowlands. Street children 'fully exemplify the permeability and inter-changeableness of the borderlines between day and night, living and non-living, public and private, or order and disorder' (ibid: 159). Also often accused of witchcraft, street children establish bridges between different worlds, overcoming dichotomies. The youth is moving in time and space, living in an environment characterised by its mobile nature.

An idea of constant movement and exchanges also exists between worlds. In witchcraft, sorcery and healing contacts are established between realms, with entities in the shadowlands presenting the power to navigate through boundaries and frontiers. Moreover, these liminal individuals present the capacity to travel long distances, with cases of witches able to travel to Europe through the night and come back during the day (De Boeck and Plissart 2004). In rituals, questions of movement are also broached. Indeed, by moving to a discursive space, to the ritual house, individuals and healers, sorcerers or witches create a new space-time that permits a multiplicity of being, inserting themselves into new temporalities and new spaces.

Finally, at the border between countries, mobility also plays a pivotal role, with constant processes of transmigration. The diamond trade implies a neverending movement between the DRC and Angola, creating a space of exchanges, contacts and incompleteness. Logics are colliding and interweaving. The violence emanating from the diamond trade inspires stories of death and chaos, with a constant threat of dislocation and dispossession (De Boeck and Plissart 2004). People at the border are often deterritorialised, far from their home, in an everlasting process of migration.

Along dislocations, the dispossession presented in the diamond trade may take the form of dismemberments. Both on a social and physical scale, corporeal dismemberment is also present in collective imaginary (De Boeck and Plissart 2004). A parallel can be established with Amos Tutuola's book *The Palm-Wine Drinkard*, in which one of the characters gathers different limbs from others through his journey to the village. He appears as a complete gentleman when reaching the marketplace, while he is a mere skull when not borrowing (Tutuola 1952: 16). Through movements and contacts, he builds a new identity and overcomes the limits of his own physical body. In shadowlands, the body is central.

The body at the crossroads between shadowlands and order

For a long time, the Cartesian dichotomy between body and mind has structured studies on the body. The variation of this binary opposition is the dichotomy between nature and culture. However, the 20th century saw researchers starting 'to study the body as an integral part of society and culture' (Sokup and Dvorakova 2016: 513). Today, the body is understood as both a confined space and a site of exchange. The corporeal envelope becomes an interface with others.

Rites and therapies represent this capacity of the physical envelope to act as an intermediary. Devisch, depicting the *Mbwoolu* rite, explains the 'transitionalness' of the skin, which permits to develop new identities and ways of being. The heart and liver are also represented as sites of negotiation between different world and forces. It reminds the *Kundu*, the special gland inherited by *Kongo* sorcerers and witches that enables them to 'eat the vital essences or power of other people' (Westerlund 2006: 172). The lower body also presents particular characteristics, especially as a communicative channel between worlds and between the different bodies (physical, social, cosmic) (Devisch and Brodeur 1999). Thus, in shadowlands, the physical body permits both transitions and developments of new capacities. It is an interface for communication and exchanges.

In the *Mbwoolu* rite, 'capable of entangling the body, may also disentangle it' (Devisch and Brodeur 1999: 152), figurines appear as symbolisations of the body. Empowered with the capacity to move from a corporeal envelope to another one, individuals experiencing the rite adopt new identities through these fetishes. Then, the artefacts, which represent the various bodies of the initiated person, foster the progression through multiple identifications.

The corporeal envelope becomes a privileged stage for the enactment of fantasies. For example, the sorcerer is characterised by his polymorphism. Similar to the Trickster figure, the Yaka sorcerer depicted by Devisch overcomes the laws of the body, the limits of the shape (Devisch and Brodeur 1999. De Boeck's analysis of witches in Kinshasa also presents the body as a site for imagination. Indeed, it is through the ingestion of human flesh that individuals become witches. These shadowlands entities also leave tattoos on the body, etching witchcraft onto it. By the way, everything appears useful in the human body, with, for example, limbs used as tableware.

However, the body as shadowlands is not limited to the religious and/or the ritual field. Indeed, in the everyday life, the corporal envelope also appears in interaction with the group and the world. Qualified by Michael Lambek and

Paul Antze as the only site of the memory (Antze and Lambek 1996), the individual body is central in the framing of history. People's envelopes become sites of remembering and generating meanings. Through Tshibumba's painting, it appears clear that human bodies are pivotal in the narrative. Indeed, out of a hundred and one creations only six do not represent a human being. Moreover, by playing with forms, shapes and body sizes Tshibumba implies different interpretations. It permits to give a shape to his history, stressing particular bodies, underlining specific figures and diminishing the presence of others.

In the Congolese society, a great importance is accorded to the image that the body showcases. Depicted by De Boeck as the spectacle city, Kinshasa, although a place of extreme poverty, accords a true cult of elegance. The concept of SAPE, Society of Ambiance-Makers and Elegant People,[12] is central in the Congolese way of being. It erases boundaries between the poor and the rich. The body becomes the centre to display wealth, elegance and well-being, even though poverty and deprivation are the main economic features. The appearance permits to interact within the group and, more widely, with the rest of the world.

The body, in its material conception, is also representative of shadowlands. Indeed, the corporal envelope structures and is shaped by processes of being and becoming. Embedded in the religious, bodies are also central in the framing of history, as well as in the everyday life. Finally, as a communicative channel, the human shape

[12] Société des Ambianceurs et des Personnes Elégantes.

permits the blurring of boundaries and physical limits, establishing transitions with other dimensions.

To conclude the part, shadowlands are first understood as physical spaces – concrete places, characterised by mobility, and underlining the centrality of the body. The concept permits to understand the logics of contacts, interconnections and creativity structuring the DRC. Nevertheless, as an epistemological tool, shadowlands overcome materiality, as showcased by the blurring of the body's boundaries. Its incompleteness and the three-dimensional gaze that it proposes permit to understand being and becoming in a larger framework, unveiling new interpretations and possibilities.

Shadowlands overcome the limits of the physical

The concept of shadowlands overreaches linear structures and the realm of the physical. Blurring boundaries, the concept is entangled in different worlds and spheres, navigating in between with everlasting possibilities of renewal. Proposed as a concept to expand and incorporate the various conceptualisations of being and becoming, shadowlands are embedded in politics, in everyday life and in the religious/ritual realm. All these spheres, permeating each other, are defined through processes of transition.

Being and becoming through political transitions

The colony has often been depicted as a *space of death*, reflecting the dark side of colonialism. Both fiction and scholar studies have approached the concept to depict the violence of the colonial enterprise (Barzman-Grennan

2016; Camus 1989; Fanon 1961; Cesaire 1955). Although the postcolonial world should have proposed a solution to the morbid situation, nations have remained linked with darkness, through confusion, conflicts and death. De Boeck evokes a 'fracture inflicted by the post-colonial world' and 'disjunctions in the myths of modernity and tradition' (De Boeck and Plissart 2004: 18). Dealing with powers facing each other, wars and ethnic conflicts, the postcolonial situation appears as a post-mortem situation. Shadowlands have succeeded one another, reinforcing the incompleteness and constant renewal of the concept.

In the case of the postcolonial DRC (Zaire at first), communities' ways of being and becoming have faced contradicting logics. *Métissages* occurred, with people who did not belong firmly to one space, who crossed social and racial lines (De Boeck and Plissart 2004). Different opportunist figures of power have seized the leadership of the nation, implementing their own conception of government and imagination of the state. De Boeck further defines the state as a black hole of power, existing but not working (ibid). The process of transition has not been smooth, rather complex and by trials and errors. Indeed, it is still ongoing, linking directly transitions and shadowlands through their unfinished nature.

During his reign from 1965 to 1997, Mobutu undertook an important process of legitimisation of his power. He implemented the 'return to authenticity', which appealed to the manipulation of traditions (De Boeck and Plissart 2004: 88). Through different processes, he intended to unify the broad mosaic of people dwelling between the borders of the nation. By granting himself numerous titles and nicknames, he reinforced his symbolic capital, using the idea of tradition and authenticity to maintain his image. His numerous regalia (leopard hat, magic stick, etc) permitted to increase his power and legitimacy, mobilising symbols and the imagination of his people. These political artefacts reactivated an ideal political space, in which the leader could blossom as a legitimate ruler. Moreover, by promoting songs, dances and cultural representations he ambiguously navigated between traditions and modernity, between changes and continuity. The public sphere appeared as a medium to showcase and legitimate the national power. Political representations were intertwined with cultural performances and shows. Mobutu's reign was also characterised by a juggling between nationalism and collaboration with the outside world. The 'return to authenticity' advocated was mainly a manipulation of traditions, blurring dichotomies and confusing his people through public apparitions and mediatisation of the political sphere. Through this perspective, Mobutu became a Trickster, a figure of shadowlands. As a charismatic leader, he stressed his role as a guide, reinforcing his Trickster and god-like image, a figure that helps to guide individuals through spaces and phases of transition (Johnston 1991).

Traditional chiefs share the same characteristics and logics of legitimisation, reactivating an ideal political space through regalia and re-actualising their power through dances and ceremonies (Devisch and Brodeur 1996). Héritier Mambi Tunga-Bau's thesis analyses the relation between traditional and state powers. His work focuses on the hybridisation of political powers in the establishment of a 'modern state in DRC' (Mambi Tunga-Bau 2010: 15). Through the different regimes (colonial, dictatorial, democratic) the state has mobilised traditional authorities to legitimise its global leadership. For example, under the AFDL (Alliance of Democratic Forces for the Liberation of Congo-Zaire), which brought Laurent Desire Kabila to power, a new mission was attributed to the traditional chief. He became responsible for the popular power committees (CPP). Although ephemeral, this regime used traditional authorities to reinforce and legitimise itself (ibid).

On the other hand, these traditional authorities have found ways to maintain their power and relevance in a transitional and modern context. Although changes have occurred, traditional authorities have persisted through decades, raising the question of the relevance of the dichotomy between change and continuity. Thus, a chief revoked by the state cannot engage with the national power anymore, however, to his people, the traditional chief stays legitimate and continues to rule in defiance of the national order. Therefore, the government has a keen interest to engage in diplomatic relationships with traditional authorities. An ongoing dialectic exists between local traditional authorities and national political order, dialectics that goes both ways. Frontiers between the local and the global, modernity and traditions appear to be blurred, exceeding binary oppositions, mainly established by the Western framework of knowledge. Moreover, a resurgence of these traditional authorities is seen in the DRC, with former monarchies restored. Today, people with high social rank even aspire to chieftaincy (Mambi Tunga-Bau 2010). Traditional authorities have renewed themselves, re-actualising their pertinence in the new sociopolitical context, resuming the metaphor of the shadowlands through its incompleteness and unfinished nature.

As seen with Mobutu, cultural politics have been mobilised to legitimise the national power. However, it is also an enterprise aiming to challenge the system, blurring the dichotomy between structure and agency. Politics becomes the field of artists, who are able to impact on governments, especially with their importance in the public, popular realm. Thus, during Mobutu's eviction from power, radios played one of Wenge Musica's songs. It mocked the fleeing dictator, linking him with a French movie villain, Fantomas (White 2008: 2). Through music, political messages were transmitted, opposing and discrediting the state and its leaders.

On the other hand, many musicians were doubtful about this power transition. Indeed, Mobutu's system rewarded artists 'for making public displays of loyalty' (ibid: 2). Strategies had been developed to negotiate between the people and the political system, with musicians being at the junction, in the shadowlands of the dichotomy system/agency. Embodiments of a dual role, artists performed in order to challenge the regime while, at the same time, introduced themselves within the logic of the governing power. 'Franco offered a perfect example of this paradox. He is remembered both as the musician who most criticised the abuses of Zaire's political bourgeoisie and as the official *griot* of the M.P.R' (ibid: 240). Today, in the context of chaos and crisis that continues to structure the DRC, music is still relevant. Indeed, 'popular dance music in Kinshasa is an excellent example of the privileged form of cultural expression that becomes instrumental in the articulation of national identities' (White 2008: 8).

Overall, the 'modern state', as seen through the Western lens, does not work. It has failed. Sometimes linked to witchcraft, colonial modernity is depicted as poisoned (De Boeck and Plissart 2004: 85). Congolese people re-appropriate the idea of the modern, nourishing it from their imagination and creativity. 'To do politics' becomes for everyone, implying an idea of being and becoming not only in relation to structure but in the everyday life, as quasi-events.

Being and becoming in the everyday life

The shadowlands are characterised by ambivalence. They are both separated and imbricated into being and reality, embodying the shadow metaphor. Being and becoming become an everyday project implicated in every interaction. 'It is not limited to special or marginalized expressive spaces, but rather also extends to the taken-for-granted and ordinary mental work, interactions, and spaces where being-becoming negotiation takes place'.[13]

In the DRC, a crisis of meaningfulness appears due to the excessive production of signs and meanings. Everyday life enters a world of shadow and darkness, confronted to chaos, creating choices and potentialities for responses. In Kinshasa, 'distinctions between urban and rural realities, between modern and traditional worlds, or between what is situated locally and what is considered to be global, can no longer be taken for granted' (De Boeck and Plissart 2004: 41). Indeed, local logics of hunting are permeating the city, both metaphorically and practically. Bars and pubs are redefined as villages, infusing the rural into the urban. The city is re-fashioned, generating a new social environment.

---

[13] See Chapter 1, p. 44.

Similar to politics, public and private spheres are interwoven in everyday life. Rumours and gossips 'constantly fracture and reshape the composite anatomy of the city's public and private spaces' (ibid: 52). It implies the creation of 'public' private spaces and 'private' public spaces. Being and becoming for Kinois become a negotiation and articulation of several simultaneous identities, encompassing both the individual and the collective. These gossips are especially drawing from the imagination of people. Popular culture becomes pivotal in this logic.

Through Papa Wemba's songs and shows children have entered the stage of the popular culture. In public spaces such as the television, movies and comic strips they have become central characters, stimulating the imagination of the people, instigating urban mythology and provocation. 'Children and youngsters appear as the ultimate focal points of the contemporary Central African imaginary. Children, as *opus operatum* and as *modus operandi* of crisis and renewal, form the identity locations in which the ruptures and faultiness of an African world in transition become manifest' (De Boeck and Plissart 2004: 158).

Street children appear as embodiments of the articulation of quasi-events in the chaotic situation of Congo. Living in markets, crossroads, abandoned railways, the youth are both relegated to sites of exclusion and prominently present in urban public spaces. By re-appropriating the city, they redefine their conception of the modern, building alternative ways of living, reshaping the city according to their rule. They develop creativity and new possibilities in chaotic situations of shadowlands. Not as vulnerable as the Western-centric framework of thought imagine them, children are also economically independent, especially in the context of the diamonds trade in which they become the 'children of Luanda'. Finally, in the space of the street, which also represents the time-space of the night, children are often linked with witchcraft. They change form, travel long distances and, thus, blur boundaries. Children present the Trickster's characteristics, establishing their own rules and laws, implying a societal and etiological crisis (De Boeck and Plissart 2004).

Youth is also pivotal in the kinship system. Profound shifts have occurred with the mingling of urban and rural logics, creating new regimes of kinship. The system of family ties witnesses a break with former concepts, blurring the relationships between kin and non-kin, inside and outside, endogamy and exogamy. In this context, children appear simultaneously as mediums and actors in the creation and development of relations and alliances. Indeed, the youth, establishing their own rules, have developed new alternative marriages and new systems of alliances. The deconstruction and shifts of kinship patterns are accompanied by changes in the system of gift, reciprocity and exchange (ibid 2004).

A memory crisis is also perceptible among the Congolese. Reflected through Mobutu's process of return to authenticity, the crisis implies that memory becomes a sense of loss, a site of death and shadow. Indeed, history and memory are neither accessible to the population nor objective. These historical gaps create processes of individual and communal re-framing and the re-appropriation of narratives around the past, with possibilities for mythologising it (ibid 2004). It continues the constant fragmentation and re-composition of the world of the Congolese, stressing the ambivalence between chaos and creativity linked with shadowlands. History becomes a process of selection, concerning both forgetting and remembering, implicating the state and the elements composing it. Again, it blurs the separation between structure and agency, reinforcing the shadowlands character of the DRC's chaotic situation.

Resuming Antze and Lambek's proposition of the individual body to serve as the only site of memory (Antze and Lambek 1996) permits to link the idea of medicine and healing with memory. Ruptures, erasures and erosions have been at stake in healing practices. Nevertheless, new syncretic forms of healing have been established, reinventing the ritual space of divination, reintroducing people in a new time-space. In shadowlands, healing practices are constantly renewed, implying an idea of incompleteness. Hybrid practices, which have supplanted older divinatory processes, are negotiations between the traditional and the modern concepts of well-being. In the field, processes of being and becoming concern both practices and the individuals within.

It is especially through New Indigenous Churches that new healing practices are developed. Sessions of deliverance and soul healing are central to counter child witches and the violence that they carry. Both undertaking to undermine imagination around witches and making it more central focusing on them, contradictory dialogic raises in churches. These institutions become spaces in which witchcraft is developed as well as possible solutions to its propagation. Neither part of it nor external, these churches appear as shadowlands, in which good and evil, Jesus Christ and witches are mingling. Emerging as a part of the everyday life by emphasising the 'power of the Holy Spirit in the daily life' (Ukah 2016: 362), these Pentecostal churches are pivotal in the social organisation of the Congolese, structuring their imagination and their possibilities of responses to the chaotic contexts faced.

Thus, the DRC's situation of shadowlands is not limited to 'meaningful' choices and negotiations with structures. It can be expanded to parcels of the everyday life, to 'insignificant events'. Shadowlands reintroduce the significance of *quasi*-events, blurring the dichotomy between structure and agency. Separations between worlds are erased, stressing the relational aspect of the shadowlands situation. This aspect is especially embodied through rites and healing practices. A particular focus on the ritual inclination of the shadowlands is the point of the last part.

Rites to renew one's identity

Rites have been intensively analysed through the prism of liminality. Overcoming the limitations of Turner's perception of the concept, such as the completeness of being and becoming and the linearity attached to the liminal metaphor,[14] I propose to analyse rites through the prism of the shadowlands. This part is based on the *Mbwoolu* rite, the enthronement rite, and Yaka funerary practices, all three presented by Devisch in his book *The Law of the Lifegivers* (1999). Indeed, by quoting the anthropologist, Brodeur explains that 'the entire phenomenology of Yaka culture is based upon the notion of threshold, margin or boundary' (Devisch and Brodeur 1999: 117). The articulation between

[14] See Chapter 1.

these 'threshold, margin or boundary' structures the society depicted and takes all its importance in rites.

First, therapies and rites in general permit to bring an important remodelling of the patient's identity. A new space-time beyond the original social order and its social codes is created, in which the patient's body and identity, as well as his kin and relationships, are interwoven. Indeed, the healer leads the patient and the community as a whole into a world overreaching the everyday social life. Rites and therapies re-establish the body, the group and the life-world (Devisch and Brodeur 1999). These practices are qualified as 'descent into hell between two points' (ibid: 156), with ideas of rebirth, regeneration and new being inherent and represented by the numerous metaphors and symbolisations of the maternal womb, the intrauterine life, and the role of the maternal uncle.

The *Mbwoolu* rite, a healing practice, embodies these characteristics. Mobilising the whole village in order to heal, the rite allows the patient to move from a disabled state to acquire a new social status, passing through various phases. Ideas of separation from the social order followed by the gestation and finally the re-birth are central, remodelling the different bodies (physical, social, cosmological) of the initiated. Paradoxical and transgressive, the rite is in the shadowlands, acting as a transitional process. Music and rhythm contribute to the transition, as both zones of separation and contacts. Music, dance and chant permit the mingling of the body, sensations, emotions and the community, as a moment of fusion between the world of the self and the world of the other. Finally, figurines used during the rite are symbols of the various states of the patient, allowing him for a new identification by transferring his essence through the artefacts. 'In his interaction with these cult figurines, which is both tactile and corporal, as well as verbal and visual, the patient explores a multiplicity of human figures and spectacular modes of identification' (ibid: 152–153). Claude Brodeur (Devisch and Brodeur 1999), in his psychoanalytic analysis of Devisch's ethnography, adds that the therapy ends when the healer authorises the patient to retie the various bonds that he has unknotted through the ritual process.

The enthronement of the chief, or investiture rite, is also considered as a transition, a rite of passage. Three phases, seclusion, handing over of coercive power to his officiants, then a few days later, to the whole community, constitute the ceremony. Again, different levels are interconnected, going beyond binary logics. Devisch proposes a ternary logic in the enthronement, implying an idea of circularity over linearity (ibid: 192). It roots the rites in shadowlands as a response to the limitations of liminality, crossroads and borderlands, which are all bounded in metaphors of lines and completeness. Bringing the integration of opposing terms, the chief espouses the logic of the monstrous. Centre of everything, he is empowered with animal dispositions, as a Trickster figure. Finally, the investiture is both symbolic and performative. The rite and the various prohibitions that go along present the characteristic of an 'invasion of disorganisation, unbinding, insofar as a series of basic relations are untied and fundamental distinction blurred' (ibid: 178).

In funeral rites, a rupture followed by a re-articulation of social bonds and limits are also at the foundation. The burial aims to disconnect the physical body of the dead from his social identity. Death also perturbed the articulation between the three bodies of the mourner. Moreover, the integrity of the whole community is threatened, in a situation of chaos. It produces a state of uncertainty, an uncanny space-time of disintegration. Mourners, during the first stage of funerary practices, are no longer implicated in social relations. The purpose of funerary rites is also to limit the contamination of death, guiding the now wandering spirit to the other world. A parallel with crossroads can be established through this idea of contamination. The concept of shadowlands continuing the possibilities of the crossroads, the metaphor of shadowlands suits the situation. More, fumigation rites compose the burial, as well as the widow's prohibitions to start a fire and to see the daylight. These phases of isolation and coldness appear as metaphorical shadowlands. Ultimately, the funerary wake turns night into day and reintroduces a demarcation between life and death, re-establishing limits and boundaries. The funeral rite permits to move out of the chaos, to overcome shadowlands.

Conclusion

Coming out of the shadow

To conclude that focus on the numerous shadowlands situations in the DRC, I have decided to analyse briefly what the logics are for coming out of this uncanny space-time.

Through the history of the country, various ambiguous situations arise. Ethnic conflicts, confusion of power, but also interactions, contacts and creativity shaped the narratives gathered. Today, the country is still facing numerous conflicts, popular uprisings and tensions, reinforcing the incompleteness of the transitional process, as well as the pertinence of the concept of shadowlands to analyse the nation. Interactions appear pivotal in the DRC's history, making central contacts and relationships in the framing of the Congolese identity. It also implies ideas of creativity, possible borrowing and new opportunities.

Shadowlands are first presented as embedded in materiality. They are places, in which mobility is central and structuring. The place of the body becomes pivotal, as a zone of transition and communicative channel. By re-shaping their environment, re-appropriating spaces, rules and logics formerly irrelevant, members of the community develop potentialities to come out of these uncanny places, or to blossom within, navigating at their will.

Moreover, the analytical tool presented expands beyond the physical world, leading to the mingling of different worlds, conceptions and binary oppositions. The political sphere, the everyday life and the rites are social spaces in which shadowlands appear frequently. Clearly, all these fields should be considered as tightly interwoven. Figures emerge from the blurriness of shadowlands, either reintroducing a similar chaotic situation or trying to re-establish a strong social order. They either blossom in the chaotic situation (children, diamonds traders, Ngafula inhabitants, sorcerers, witches, etc) or establish medium to move on (*Mbwoolu* rite, healers, churches, political figures, etc..). In healing practices, oracles resume these potentialities that grow in the shadow, aiming at the 'reinsertion of disorder into an order of language and exchange which serve as the foundation of life and society' (Devisch and Brodeur 1999: 112). The articulation between structure and agency becomes blurred, with a constant negotiation leading the possible responses.

Shadowlands are complex spaces, ambivalent, sharing simultaneously chaotic characteristics and possibilities for new opportunities and development. They permit to redefine being and becoming, through the incompleteness and the multidimensional gaze inherent. In the DRC, which faces an everlasting process of transition, they are particularly relevant at every layer of the society. Political figures, but also religious, mythical and popular entities can emerge. Shadowlands, in which rules and laws are abrogated, become spaces for opportunists and opportunism.

Personal take-away

First and foremost, my interest in the DRC and its specific situation comes from past works, including one that I realised on Mobutu during my undergraduate studies in France. I found the complex figure that he embodies particularly interesting and his attempt to legitimise his power through the mobilisation of cultural politics relatively ambiguous. Moreover, the network of relationships that I built with Congolese people since my arrival in South Africa has reinforced my interest.

Not totally aware of the situation as I started my readings on the subject, I have found, through chapter and articles, an important amount of crisis and chaotic situations that justified an approach through the metaphor of the shadowlands. The unfinished nature of the transition and the multilayered and complex situations of the DRC embody the main features of the shadowlands: the incompleteness and the three-dimensional, nonlinear approach.

With more time and a larger corpus, I could have expanded some parts of my work. For example, economic factors could have been analysed more deeply, reintroducing shadowlands of globalism and neoliberalism that many African countries face. The kinship system could also have been developed, with an analysis on the logics of reciprocity, gift and exchange. However, either my pieces did not present these subjects in-depth or, sometimes, choices had to be made. Anthropology and theorisation are subjective processes that need the creation of a specific space. They cannot aim for completeness or exhaustiveness. Similar to shadowlands, anthropology and theorisation are incomplete, constantly embedded in situations of renewals.

Finally, the research has been very interesting. I have enlarged my knowledge on the DRC, linking it to a concept that the group and myself have developed from scratch. I enjoyed the analysis, especially Tshibumba's historical narrative (Fabian 1996) and White's connections between popular music and politics (2008). In further work, I aim to carry on the concept of shadowlands, deconstructing dichotomies and undertaking an approach that challenges the Western-centric framework of thought. It would insert my studies in a decolonial intellectual framework. As an epistemological tool, shadowlands unveil new ways to do research, focusing more on contacts and interactions. Studies become more dynamic, liberating interpretations and potentialities. In my Master research that focuses on the negotiation between the KhoeSan indigenous identity and the Rasta identity, the concept could be a useful tool. Indeed, the frontier between the two identities studied emerges as fluid and characterised by its porosity. This leads to great possibilities for adaptation, borrowing, exchange and renewal. Boundaries are blurred, strict separations erased and chaotic situations overcome. Therefore, the concept of shadowlands can define this particular experience as well as being a tool to help understand it.

References

Antze, P. and Lambek, M. (1996) *Tense Past: Cultural Essays in Trauma and Memory*, New York: Routledge.

Barzman-Grennan, A. (2016) 'The Space of Death: The Black Hole from Which Colonialism Emerges', in *Colonialism and the Making of the Modern World* (Seminar).

Bazin, J. (1979) 'La Production d'un Récit Historique', in *Cahiers d'études Africaines*, No. 73, pp. 435–83.

Camus, A. (1989) *The Stranger*, New York: Vintage International.

Césaire, A. (2000 [1955]) *Discourse on Colonialism*, New York: Monthly Review Press.

De Boeck, F. and Plissart, MF. (2004) *Kinshasa: Tales of the invisible city*, Leuven: Leuven University Press.

De Boeck, F. (2010) *Cemetery State* (Documentary), Rumst: FilmNatie.

Devisch, R. and Brodeur, C. (1999) *The Law of the Lifegivers: The Domestication of Desire*, Amsterdam: Harwood Academic Publishers.

Fabian, J. (1996) *Remembering the Present: Painting and Popular History in Zaire*, Berkeley: University of California Press.

Fanon, F. (1963 [1961]) *The Wretched of the Earth*, New York: Grove Press.

Johnston, S. (1991) 'Crossroads', *Zeitschrift fur Papyrologie und Epigraphik*, No. 88, pp. 217–24.
Mambi Tunga-Bau, H. (2010) *Pouvoir Traditionnel et Pouvoir d'Etat en R*
epublique Democratique du Congo. Doctoral Thesis, Kinshasa: Mediapaul.
Soukup, M. and Dvorakova, M. (2016) 'Anthropology of body: The Concept Illustrated on an Example of Eating Disorder', in *Slovak Ethnology*, Vol. 4, No. 64, pp. 513–29.
Tutuola, A. (1961 [1952]) *The Palm-Wine Drinkard and His Dead Palm-Wine Tapster in the Dead's Town*, London: Faber and Faber.
Ukah, A. (2016) 'The Deregulation of Piety in the Context of Neoliberal Globalization: African Pentecostalisms in the Twenty-First Century', in V. Synan, A. Yong and K. Asamoah-Gyadu, *Global Renewal Christianity*, Florida: Charisma House, pp. 362–79.
Westerlund, D. (2006) 'Witchery among the Sukuma, Kongo and Yoruba', in *African Indigenous Religions and Disease Causation*, Leiden: Brill, pp. 165–88.
White, B. W. (2008) *Rumba Rules: The Politics of Dance Music in Mobutu's Zaire*, Durham: Duke University Press.

Printed in the United States
By Bookmasters